Towards a New Kind of Building

CREDITS

This publication was made possible by the generous support of
Delft University of Technology, Faculty of Architecture

Further substantial donations were given by
Arcadis, BAM Infraconsult, Heijmans and NPC ExpertCenter

Photos credits are embodied in the captions.

Author: **Kas Oosterhuis**
Design: **Studio Léon&Loes**
Printing: **Die Keure, Bruges**
Paper: **inside arctic volume highwhite 115 gr/m²**
Cover: **invercote G wit 350 gr/m²**
Production: **NAi Publishers, Rotterdam**
Project coordination: **Alma Timmer, Marcel Witvoet, NAi Publishers**
Publisher: **Eelco van Welie, NAi Publishers, Rotterdam**

NAi Publishers is an internationally orientated publisher specialized in developing, producing and distributing books on architecture, visual arts and related disciplines. www.naipublishers.nl

Available in North, South and Central America through D.A.P./Distributed Art Publishers Inc, 155 Sixth Avenue 2nd Floor, New York, NY 10013-1507, tel +1 212 627 1999, fax +1 212 627 9484, dap@dapinc.com

Available in the United Kingdom and Ireland through Art Data, 12 Bell Industrial Estate, 50 Cunnington Street, London W4 5HB, tel +44 208 747 1061, fax +44 208 742 2319, orders@artdata.co.uk

Printed and bound in Belgium
ISBN 978-90-5662-763-8

Towards a New Kind of Building

> *Tag*
> *Make*
> *Move*
> *Evolve*

KAS OOSTERHUIS
NAi PUBLISHERS

1. >*Tag That Body*

all building components will be tagged as to process information

2. >*Shape That Body*

the point cloud is organized by powerlines to shape the body

3. >*Move That B*●*dy*

building components are actors in a complex adaptive system

4. >*Evolve That B*●*dy*

the building body is a personal universe living inside evolution

PREFACE

Alea Iacta Est! New Bodies for Architecture

Kas Oosterhuis is one of the few architects in the world who has 'crossed the Rubicon'. For Kas, the die has been cast, and work must be made *Towards a New Kind of Building*. Oosterhuis has built a solid outpost, expressive and credible, on the far shore of a radically new architecture. This position constitutes a benchmark for all those who currently believe in the need for a revolution linked with the affirmation of the IT paradigm. At the same time, his work is also a reference point for all of contemporary architecture.

What are the key elements of this position? The first component is the presence of a series of actually constructed works that concretely demonstrate these new principles. These include historically significant buildings such as the 1997 Saltwater Pavilion at Neeltje Jans, the Netherlands (one of the first interactive buildings in the world), the Garbage Transfer Station in Zenderen, or the Web of North-Holland pavilion. But one of these major works stands out as a real masterpiece of recent architecture: the Cockpit in the Acoustic Barrier, an infrastructural system that acts as an acoustic barrier then transforms as it progresses to become a real building.

   This sound-absorbing structure is defined as it shifts and changes across the landscape and performs more than one function: an acoustic infrastructure, protection from wind, a potential solar collector and environmental purification system, and finally an actual building. By recoiling and folding in on itself, the barrier also creates the environments for an elegant automobile showroom with a garage annex, and then rolls out to once again become a screen and acoustic barrier. This construction gives a new vision of a series of themes permeating all architectural research over the past few years. This is clear proof that even those who do not truly believe in the ideas of Oosterhuis cannot disregard the architectural value this work has achieved.

But the ability to put major buildings on the field is only the first of the components in Oosterhuis's position. The second component is the university research he carries out at the Hyperbody institute he founded in 2000 at Delft University of Technology. This institute performs research, builds prototypes, publishes reviews, organizes conferences and involves teachers and doctoral students in the more complex aspects of theoretical research, as well as hundreds of students in education. All this happens at the gates of Rotterdam, a city well known for its architectural vitality, and home to the Netherlands Architecture Institute (NAI), one of the pulsating centres for the promotion and diffusion of architecture culture worldwide.

In addition to this university research, the third component is naturally the ONL studio founded with his wife Ilona Lénárd, an integral part of an extremely close-knit, wonderfully cooperative association with Kas. Ilona's work constantly energizes the relationship between professional development and artistic research. The challenges of active design are handled with such power of persuasion as to lead across to this far shore consultants, technology suppliers, and above all clients who, along with collaborators, are guided by Oosterhuis and Lénárd into a new concept of building to face and resolve practically, and frequently ingeniously, all aspects connected with an architecture radically different than the traditional.

So what has been missing in this position? What has been lacking is a book that would be the synthesis, the promise, and above all the perspective of this approach. And this has finally arrived; you are holding it: *Towards a New Kind of Building*. As you may know, over the past few years Oosterhuis has actually done quite a bit of writing, including elegant and perfectly illustrated volumes of his works, as well as collections of articles and essays, miscellaneous substantial volumes on conferences he has organized, and books with a theoretical theme such as *Hyperbodies in the IT Revolution in Architecture* book series.

But the book you have here is at a much higher level than this earlier work, and holds great interest in the structure, information and examples of many buildings, prototypes and projects created by ONL or other designers. In fact, the original and particularly successful aspect of this work lies in the interplay between theory, design and concrete examples.

Written by Oosterhuis, this book is organized into four large sections that use the analogy of the body to help understand the new architecture. The first section is called 'Tag That Body'. What does this mean? This means that all the components of a building can potentially be tagged; that is, they are recognizable parts of the system. Consider actually incorporating RFIDs (Radio Frequency IDentifications), already quite inexpensive, into the various components of a building. In this arrangement, the components become identifiable, nameable, personalizable, each different and above all activatable... as if each were an actual being. What is the potential behaviour of this tagged-body-building? First and foremost, *it is to move in a swarm*; that is, the various parts share several rules with their neighbours and have local micro-behaviours and macro group behaviours! You might say, 'This is crazy!' But remember the first lines of this introduction. This approach is no mere futuristic theory; ONL actually creates and builds these things.

The second large section of this book is called 'Shape That Body' and describes how this new type of building is logically designed, the rules it follows, and forms it can logically take. A series of fundamental ideas for Oosterhuis come into play in this section. For example, 'one building, one detail', or the lengthened development of structures that have a head and a tail to manage a series of inputs and outputs, or a series of analogies with the design and construction of cars.

The third part is called 'Move That Body' and more fully develops the fundamental idea connected with the principle of interactivity; that is, the fact that the building is constantly reconfigurable, a 'physical' reconfigurability according to Oosterhuis. In other words, the building actually moves in order to change with the modification of functional, environmental and contextual conditions, and finally to experience the general condition *of desire* as a field that brings architecture into the dynamic, living world of plants and animals, rather than the static world of stone.

The fourth section, 'Evolve That Body', instead deals with the lines of development and reasoning anticipated by this new type of building, which may incorporate new technological advances on the verge of breaking into the world of construction. Consider the use in construction of nanotechnologies, File-to-Factory or Computer Numeric Control; Kas feels these are all part of a reality already widely tested, but they have yet to generally permeate the work of design and production.

In this last section, the author brings to life his way of thinking and, of great interest for the reader, explicitly attacks other architectural positions; some of these positions are in his field of IT research (for example, his approach is quite distant from an idea of 'Blob Architecture' and is naturally closer to the work of architects like Marcos Novak, Patrick Schumacher or Makoto Sei Watanabe), and some positions in postconstructive architecture, particularly the opinions of Koolhaas from whom he clearly distances himself. In short, Kas uses these differences to show us he is already, as we said at the beginning, on the far shore of a new idea in architecture. He writes:

My personal design universe consists of interacting populations of groups of points in space, wirelessly connected by force fields that are aware of themselves, communicating with their immediate neighbours... My design universe includes interacting point clouds, in which each point behaves as if it is the centre of the world, even though it is just 'somewhere', as our Earth is just somewhere in the Milky Way... Each point is an actor, always busy measuring and adjusting its position in relation to its peers. Each point is an actuator, triggering the execution of its internal program. Each point is an IPO, a receiver, processor and sender in one. Each point of my personal design point cloud displays behaviour, it has character and style. Each point of the point cloud is a microscopic instrument to be played, a game to be unfolded.

The final part of this book provides a place for reflections on quantum mechanics, connected with a series of studies, lectures and research projects. The quantum world proceeds by leaps and bounds and not slow transformations, a world where opposite positions coexist along with a method of studying phenomena in a manner extremely close to the non-pre-established organization of every living being, since it is in fact *probabilistic*. At this point, it is clear why quantum theory greatly involves the new type of architecture being constructed by Kas Oosterhuis and thus postulates the construction of a quantumBIM (a Building Information Model 'dealing with the principles of uncertainty and unpredictability').

I am particularly interested in discussing the point in which the author of a book dedicated to the application of quantum mechanics to Urban Design – *Quantum City* by Ayssar Arida – describes two ways of concretely applying quantum theory (or in reality any other scientific theory) to the field of design. One is by way of modelling; the other is via metaphorization. Naturally Kas, also a builder and an architect extremely attentive to the concrete resolution of the interactive system of components he designs, has a great suspicion of any vague ideas of metaphorization (the use of a scientific theory as a 'generic' form of inspiration). Kas clearly works, and continues to work, to produce real 'modelling', that is, the mathematical extrapolation of several fundamental connections between quantum mechanics and his Hyperbodies (that is then a method of describing this new type of building, but you already understand this).
In his book, Arida presents both ways, but then in one step (page 119) realizes one fundamental characteristic. Quantum theory, as opposed to other scientific theories, *shares several principles with the metaphor itself.* In particular the principle of complementarity; that is, 'both/and' logic exists in quantum theory. In other words, elements can be modified by evolving in one direction or another. Although this observation is not further developed in Arida's book, it is a crucial question to Kas Oosterhuis.

Let's try and understand. From the beginning of the IT Revolution in Architecture series, the role of metaphor in creating a new generation of architecture is seen as one of the driving engines of a new architecture. In 1998 (in *Hyperarchitettura*, the afterword to the first book in the series) I wrote: 'Can we develop an architecture that is not only metaphorical, but also a "creator of metaphors," that leaves its own decodification open, free, structured/non-structured, and suggests and presents the user with the possibility of 'making his own story?'
In other words, the real end of the new architecture is not only first level metaphorization (a museum that recalls the presence of a ship for example), but that of a second, higher level. Shouldn't we be able not only to imagine a fluid, metaphorical, open architecture that plays off skins as new, immaterial sensors, that encompasses and treasures a multimediality that pushes into systems of control and information, but is above all capable of generating and causing to be generated other metaphors, ones with a decodification not rigidly pre-set but 'probabilistically' open? Can we not work with this ambitious and difficult idea as a frontier in our efforts?'

At this point readers will say to themselves, the writer of this preface (along with Kas) is crazy! What have second-level metaphors, quantum theory and the directions of new architecture got to do with each other? But if you consider it, you will understand. The entire construction of classic science was deterministic, absolute, cause and effect. Quantum mechanics is instead 'probabilistic'. As in real life itself, there is a lower or higher probability that any event will happen. In life, not in plants and even less in animals, no event is given as certain, but only as a probability. So in the field of aesthetic and poetic knowledge, the metaphor answers to the same probabilistic rule! A metaphor narrows, directs a way of looking or doing or interpreting, never deterministically closes, but only narrows, *accelerates* the field of convergences. In other words, works like a swarm that goes in one direction, not an assembly line or military march.

The relationship between quantum thought applied to the architecture and work of Kas Oosterhuis, who theorizes, designs and teaches how to create this new architecture, in the end introduces a new unforeseen direction and a new higher level. Quantum mechanics shares the same basic characteristics of the metaphor. The metaphor is quantum, and therefore quantum theory (one of the most important scientific theories whose potential has yet to be completely explored) also explains the existence of a divergent thought, unexpected, in the minority, the thought of aesthetic knowledge.

Art at this point could be seen, like probability, non-predominant, but when it happens it reveals a new path, the path that discovers something new by going off course! Metaphor, quantum and art share the risk, the possibility, the coincidences that are the stuff of life.

So 'Evolve That Body', you, the reader! With Kas, and his tools, his prototypes, his ideas, his pieces of software, his brilliant intuition on how to build and create this new architecture. You, the reader, architects and designers, must also experience this new direction. A solid outpost already exists for this adventure, but the territory has yet to be explored. It may be daunting and full of pitfalls, but this is the land of the future

Antonino Saggio

1.

> *Tag That Body*

all building components will be tagged as to process information

1.1 As the World Turns

The world is changing. So is architecture, the art of building, primarily due to evolving communication and manufacturing methods that have changed drastically and with increasing speed. In this book I present a theory and practice of architecture based on the principles of swarm behaviour, which builds from the provocative assumption that all building components must be designed to be active actors. I have concluded that buildings and their constituent components can no longer be seen as passive objects. This assumption revolutionizes the way we organize the design process, the way we organize the manufacturing process, and the way we interact with built structures. The new kind of building is based on the invasion of digital technologies into the building industry, such technologies as parametric design, generative components, file-to-factory production, the process of mass customization, and embedded intelligent agents. Step-by-step we are balancing the familiar top-down control with emergent bottom-up behaviour. We are rethinking the basic building blocks and we are building bottom-up bidirectional relationships between all constituent building components. I will explore the effects that the paradigm shift from mass production to mass customization will have on the designer's imagination. Once designers are open to this new reality, architecture will no longer be the same. Within 50 years this new reality will be the common language of international architects.

If my assumption proves to be false – despite all the efforts I have made over the past 20 years to develop the use of industrial customization in the realized works of our architecture office ONL [Oosterhuis_Lénárd] in Rotterdam, and, in the last decade, to develop the theory of swarm behaviour in various educational and research projects with my Hyperbody Research Group at the Faculty of Architecture of Delft University of Technology – I will be the first to acknowledge that. But if it proves to be right, I will take great pleasure in having been an early mover in the design and construction of buildings according to the new rules of industrial customization, and I will be satisfied at having explored the fascinating consequences of swarm behaviour for the profession of architecture.

001 CONNECTED

It is summer 2010, and only 14 years since I got my first cell phone using the GSM network, and only 16 years since I got my first email address at the Well, a start-up company run by Kevin Kelly in Sausalito, California. I used my first cell phone when we ran the paraSITE project in Rotterdam. My first use of the Internet was in 1994 to host the multidisciplinary event Sculpture City. I purchased my first PC, the notorious Atari 1024ST, around 1988. I used it to do three-dimensional modelling of my design for the Theo van Doesburg exhibition in Museum Boymans van Beuningen. At the same time, my partner Ilona Lénárd used the Atari to sketch intuitively, exploring early 3d programs such as STAD3d. During the years 1988 and 1989 we lived and worked in Meudon in the former studio

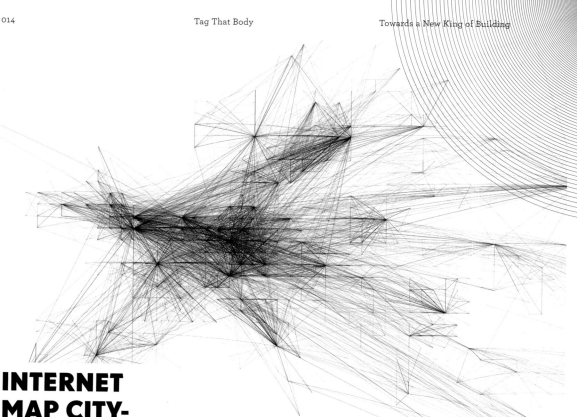

INTERNET MAP CITY-TO-CITY CONNEC-TIONS

_chrisharrison.net

of Theo van Doesburg. Before moving there, I purchased a fax-telephone machine, which cost me more than 3000 HFL, in order to communicate with the AA in London where I was unit master for Intermediate Unit 12 and with my client Evert van Straaten for the Doesburg exhibition in Rotterdam. In the late 1980s and beginning of the 1990s we became networked with the world via Internet, cell phones and fax machines. We knew instinctively that we needed to explore the potential of our new technology for art and architecture. This inspired us to organize a series of events: 'Artificial Intuition in Galerie Aedes' in Berlin and at Delft University of Technology (1990), 'Synthetic Dimension and Global Satellite in the Zonnehof' in Amersfoort (1991), 'Sculpture City in Rotterdam and the Internet' (1994), and 'Genes of Architecture' in Rotterdam, Vienna, Budapest and Berlin (1995). Once we experienced the promise of information and communications technology (ICT) in architecture and art, Ilona and I decided to build our architecture practice with the fusion of art and architecture on the digital platform, which enabled us to exchange information and raw data with practitioners of many other disciplines, such as composers, engineers and graphic designers. ONL was an early mover among the international population of architects, simply because we were interested in applying new technologies in our profession. We felt that we just had to do it, although, as we know now, we were well ahead of our time.

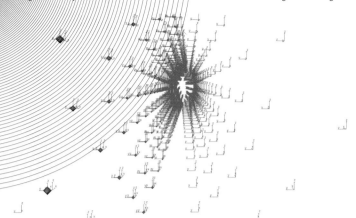

POINT CLOUD OF REFERENCE POINTS ACOUSTIC BARRIER

_ONL [Oosterhuis_Lénárd] 2004

002 POINT CLOUD ACOUSTIC BARRIER

In 1998 we were commissioned by Nora Hugenholtz of Project-bureau Leidsche Rijn to do the design of a 1.6-km-long acoustic barrier along the A2 motorway, and we were asked to think about how to represent the commercial firms behind the barrier. We applied the strategy of multiple use of the ground, and proposed to embed a substantial building within the very barrier. In fact we considered the barrier and the Cockpit building – as we proposed to name it – as one continuous structure, with a pumped up volume where it was needed for the Cockpit. Intuitively we combined many strategies into one coherent structure. Because we described the project conceptually as one unified entity, we could also take the logical next step and develop one organizational structure for the whole project, including the flat-ended and cantilevered endings and the expanded Cockpit bubble. We came up with the concept of establishing a point cloud of thousands of reference points, with each point occupying an exact position in space. This allowed us to write a script describing all constituent building components with high precision. It was unprecedented at that time, and still is unique that an architect actually controls the complex geometry in such high precision that the manufacturer – Meijers Staalbouw, in this case – could use the architect's data for the computer numerical control (CNC) production of all components: steel, glass and rubber customized to the extreme. Each and every component was different in its dimensions and its shape. The file-to-factory (F2F) process of mass customization was born and we have applied it ever since.

003 SWARM OF BIRDS

Everyone has at least once been amazed to see how birds flock in the air. Many have studied the simple rules the birds execute when flocking. The birds are constantly aware of their neighbours – avoiding collisions, keeping agreed-upon distances, adapting to their neighbour's direction, striving for a more central position in the flock. Their flocking behaviour has even been modelled in simple computer graphics. In 1986, Craig Reynolds made a computer model of animal motion (red3d.com), scripting the rules for

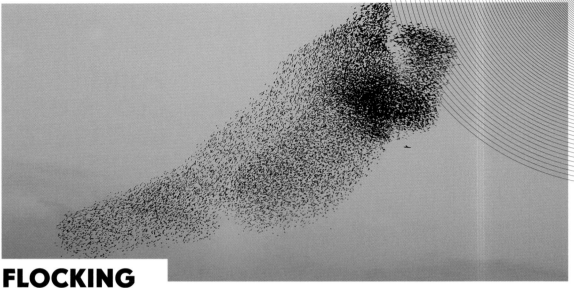

FLOCKING SPARROWS

_photo Bjarne Winkler

creatures he named 'boids', based on three-dimensional computa-tional geometry. Why then are we interested in boids and swarms of birds? Why did I introduce the term 'swarm architecture' in 2001 during the first Game Set and Match Conference I organized at Delft University of Technology (hyperbody.nl)? My objective has been clear from the beginning; I wished both then and now to treat all possible building components as interacting elements that have bi-directional relations with each other. The idea of behaviour intrigued me because it would lay the foundation for an architec-ture that is not static, but animated in real time. Animated not as described by Greg Lynn in his book Animated Form (1998), who de facto claimed his right to kill the animation, but animated in its purest meaning, keeping the structure 'informed' much like the flock of birds. I concluded that there was no reason to freeze the motion, and I realized we needed to use information and communi-cation technology (ICT) to sustain the information flow throughout the complete lifecycle of the built structure.

1.2 The Informed Point Cloud

As the world keeps turning we will need to redefine the founda-tions of architecture from time to time. Now more than 20 years have passed since the introduction of the personal computer, since the emergence of the global Internet, since the embedding of miniaturized information technology in our consumer prod-ucts. Although today we are familiar with remote control, with wireless Internet, with intelligent agents active on the Internet, with intelligent agents embedded in consumer products like printers, cars and computers, we have not yet seen much change in the very building blocks of the built environment. Neither have we seen much change in the way we design and build our environ-ment. We have, though, developed computer programs to simu-late otherwise traditional building materials like concrete, steel, glass, composites in a Building Information Model (BIM) in which the simulated building components are tagged with information about their qualitative and quantitative properties. But most architects do not use computer technology as they design. Even at respected universities students are not taught to use the computer to design. This proves once again how slow the building industry and its counterparts in the educational institutes are in catching up with new technologies. But it is not my aim to complain, on the contrary, I want to show a possible way forward – forward to the basics of the profession of architecture.

To take that step forward I imagine the built structure to be represented by a point cloud of acting reference points, points that move all the time like the birds in a swarm. The points of the point cloud are continuously informed by the receipt of streaming information as to how to behave. The points process the streaming information and the points *produce* new streaming information as do the birds in the swarm. Suppose the information defining its spatial coordinates received by the point doesn't change. Then the position of the point in the point cloud remains stable; it does

SMART DUST
_ucsd.edu

not change its position. Now suppose some data do change, then the point will act accordingly and change its position, or change any of the other properties the point has been tagged with. The crux of the new kind of building is that all reference points will be informed both during the design process and during its subsequent lifecycle. Even if we are commissioned to design for a static environment, we set up the Building Information Model (BIM) in such a way that all constituent components can potentially receive, process and send streaming information. Perhaps we should refer to the Building Information Model as 'Building in Motion'. We then will perform further research on the possibility of embedding intelligent information processing tags in all building materials so that they can be identified and addressed by wireless senders. Think, literally, of pieces of steel, concrete, glass, or composites with embedded RFID (radio-frequency identification) tags to begin with, and with microcomputers later, with a variety of actuators yet to come. During the last decade I and my Hyperbody group at Delft University of Technology have designed and built several prototypes that demonstrate the enormous potential for architecture. ONL has thus identified a promising and functional application of the theory of informed point clouds as the basic building blocks for streaming connectivity between all building components. The informed building blocks thus become actors in an environment of interacting complex adaptive systems.

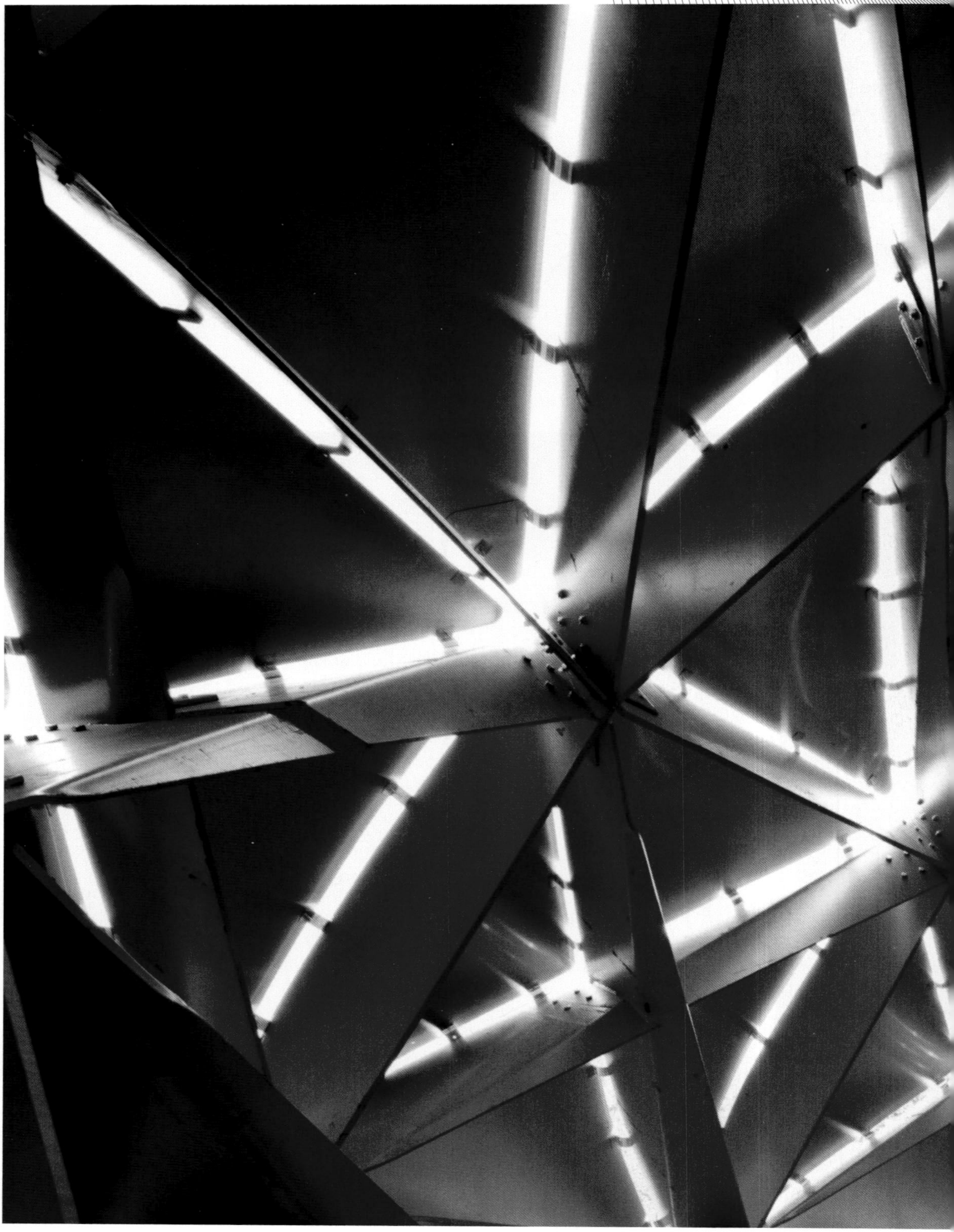

iWEB
_ONL [Oosterhuis_Lénárd]
2007 / photo Dieter Vandoren

51° 59' 49'' N
4° 22' 35'' E

1.3 Forward to Basics

This book is both a guide for daily architectural practice and a guide for researchers delving into theoretical constructs in order to push the practice forward. The underlying message of this book could very well be 'Forward to Basics', the basics being the dynamic principles of the proto building information model (protoBIM), which will be explained later. The basic building blocks of architecture need to be redefined. They are not bricks and mortar, neither are they exclusively bits and bytes. It is rather the merger of bits and atoms that interest us – the merger of the old organic real and the new real, the virtual real. One merges into the other, and vice versa. The new building blocks are informed components, hardware augmented with software mapped onto each individual building block. Each individual building block will communicate with other buildings blocks in a streaming fashion, anywhere, anytime, any way, thus requiring a radical shift to the meaning of Eisenman's ANY conferences. The new meaning takes us from a dying deconstructivism to the vibrant era of synthetic architecture, which was the not accidentally chosen title of my first solo exhibition in the Aedes Gallery in Berlin in 1990. Synthesizing architecture means redefining the very building blocks and building up a new language from scratch. Synthetic architecture has seen a sequence of evolutionary steps from liquid architecture (Marcos Novak 1991) through transarchitecture (Marcos Novak 1995) to nonstandard architecture (Frédéric Migayrou/Zeynep Mennan 2003). Nowadays it is common for students and young professionals to use Generative Components (Robert Aish/Bentley Systems), Grasshopper (Rhino plug-in), Digital Project (Gehry Technologies) or similar parametric software to synthesize the new language of architecture. ONL's contribution in this field has been to actually build, on a large scale, generated structures as early as 1997 (Waterpavilion), 2002 (WEB of North-Holland) and 2005 (Cockpit in Acoustic Barrier). ONL has effectively made the connection between the bits and the atoms and thus proven that the direction taken in the early 1990s was the right choice. This forward-looking approach has led to the new kind of building, based on thoroughly redefined genes of architecture.

Forward to basics. We go forward because we do not want to look back. We don't look in the rear-view mirror to see what is behind us, we want to look around and appreciate what we see. Now, in 2010, is the perfect time to accelerate innovation in the architecture and construction business. It is a time to rethink the basis of our society after the Internet bubble and the mortgage crisis that shook society's foundations. It is the proper time to implement streaming nonstandard customized strategies in all businesses related to the building industry, from designers to manufacturers. And speaking for myself, this is the perfect time to develop the protoBIM innovation based on the principles of swarm behaviour in order to inspire software developers to support this new kind of dynamic building. Forward to basics does not mean to step back to what we already knew 20 years ago, that would be *back* to basics. Forward to basics means redefining our core business, redefining architecture, redefining the building industry, redefining the behaviour of built structures, redefining the very essence of our profession.

004: protoCELL

protoCELL BUILDING BLOCKS FOR protoSPACE 4.0 LAB
_Hyperbody 2010 /
photo Chris Kievid

The protoSPACE lab 2.0 in the iWEB pavilion (formerly known as the Web of North-Holland) had to close down due to the 2008 fire that destroyed the Faculty of Architecture. In the spring of 2010 we opened protoSPACE 3.0 inside the walls of the new BK City on the Delft University of Technology campus. In the 2009 MSc2 course Hyperbody students designed a new protoSPACE 4.0 lab, a stand-alone pavilion between BK City and the Delft Science Centre. For protoSPACE 4.0 we developed a completely new building system based on an assemblage of large unique computer numerical control (CNC)-produced building blocks. The prototypical building block we called protoCELL. The parametric protoCELL unit comes with a series of interacting function-specific swarms: daylight swarm, artificial light swarm, ventilation swarm, interaction swarm, heating swarm, display swarm. Each featured swarm consists of 10 to 20 parametric building components. The different swarms inter-act in a loose configuration, intermingling the specified functional units, but never betraying the swarm to which the unit belongs. The units are CNC milled from polystyrene foam and coated with a strong polyurea skin. All building blocks of all swarms are both structural and provide for insulation. The hundred large building blocks of the proposed protoSPACE 4.0 fit together like the unique pieces of a 3d puzzle. The centre of gravity of the units forms the point cloud of reference points. The reference points are further specified to form the details of the geometric relations between the units. Each reference point thus becomes a group of parametrically related points.

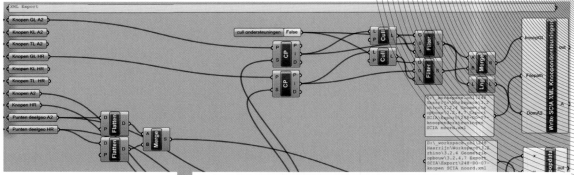

GRASS-HOPPER GRAPH HAARRIJN STRUCTURAL SYSTEM

_ONL [Oosterhuis_Lénárd]

005 GRASSHOPPER SCRIPT HAARRIJN

A typical procedure in ONL/Hyperbody designs is to define the feature lines of the whole structure first, then define the point cloud of reference points, and then augment the points with further details for the physical nodes. The data produced by the Grasshopper scripts are used directly for the CNC production of the constituent building components. The Haarrijn sound barrier features a dense stainless steel mesh along the A2 side and 6-mm solid natural suminium plates on the other side. As in all ONL designs, all sides are considered to be front sides and are treated as such. For the Haarrijn project we took the responsibility for the structural design as well. In collaboration with Arcadis we set up an immediate link between the geometry of the designer and the calculations of the structural engineer. One of the requirements for the evolutionary success of synthetic architecture is to have a direct link in the early design process among the most relevant disciplines. In the Haarrijn project we created the direct link between our Grasshopper file and the structural engineers' SCIA file. Grasshopper exports coordinates and other previously agreed upon data to XML. SCIA reads the XML file, changes some data on the basis of the calculations, and exports the new data to XML which are read again by Grasshopper. This directly facilitates a strong feedback loop between designer (geometry) and engineer (calculation). The feedback loop is iterated many times to reach the optimum in kilograms of steel, number of nodes, foundation frequency and costs.

1.4 Unique Address for Each Building Component

The essence of any designer software that interests me is seeing all constructs (buildings, installations, environments) as dynamic structures consisting of a large set of thousands of programmable components. Programmable components are individuals with unique identities, they have a unique address, in the same way all computers are assigned unique IP (Internet Protocol) addresses. Only because of this unique IP address can each individual computer be connected – both as an actor and as a receiver – to the global Internet. When a building component has an address, it can receive instructions and it can accept information that is either being pulled or being pushed from a database. Receiving, processing and sending data means that this building component becomes an actor, that it can change its configuration. Such was the invention of the ONL project Trans-Ports, beginning in 1999. The invention was to regard buildings as instrumental bodies that can change shape and content in real time. Bodies can be addressed, and all constituent components that make up the entire body can be addressed individually. The building components are like the cells in a body, small processors of information working together while constituting the building body as a whole. For example, a programmable building component could be an actuator in the form of a hydraulic cylinder with embedded sensors that make it into a structural member with the capacity to adjust its length – becoming longer or shorter – by adjusting its stroke. In the theoretical yet realizable Trans-Ports project it is calculated that only a limited number of approximately 5 x 6 = 30 programmable large actuators are needed to evoke the behaviour of the dynamic body. The skin of the body would have to be flexible with the capacity to stretch and shrink, achieved by constructing a folded skin loosely affixed to the dynamic structure. In this example the skin follows the structure. Other concepts can be imagined as well. The point I want to make here is that from the moment one starts to think of a building body as a dynamic construct, a wealth of new possibilities can appear in the designer's imagination, enticing the designer to become a pioneer again.

1.5 The Need for Nonlinear Software

To design complex and programmable buildings one needs parametric software. The concept of parametric design is in itself nothing new; it has existed for more than 30 years, originating in the shipbuilding industry. Looking more closely at the achievements of the shipbuilding industry, where the design and building task is usually to build large-scale one-offs, is useful for understanding the direction where architecture will be heading in the coming decades. Customization will be the buzz-word. Architects will base their designs on a variety of mass-customized one-offs rather than relying on the old-school serial approach of mass-produced components. This can only be achieved when we build our models in a comprehensive parametric way. Parametric design basically means the building of bidirectional relations, that is, the relations between each individual building component, with no exceptions allowed. Unfortunately, existing parametric software has its pitfalls. Suppose the designer has built a correct parametric model, but based on certain vague assumptions. Then it is very likely that the designer will have to revise the model drastically when any of the assumptions change. And that is what assumptions usually do during the intense evolution of a design concept. To avoid these drastic changes, all assumptions must be translated into parametric values. Literally every seemingly soft design act must be modelled as a hard parametric fact.

There is another pitfall; now suppose the designer switches to another design rule, changing the rules while playing. That means that the parametric model will need to be restructured, an even more drastic change in the evolution of the design. To work with changing rules during the design process we need a new species of software, one that is much less hierarchical, less linear, and more intuitive, more immediate. The relations between the components will need to be more flexible, in fact, more like the members of a dynamic swarm. Nonlinear parametric software is badly needed for information architects to be able to work more intuitively.

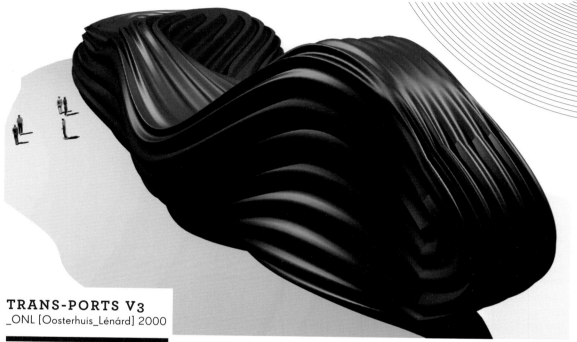

TRANS-PORTS V3
_ONL [Oosterhuis_Lénárd] 2000

1.6 Bidirectional Relationships

Let me illustrate the implications of parametric logic with a simple phrase: I put a cup of coffee on the table. When we try to describe the parametric relationships between the cup and the table, between the 'I' and the cup, between the cup and the coffee, we get very close to the nature of dynamic parametric design. From there we can make the leap towards the essence of *behavioural* design, leading towards a vision of how the new kind of building may be conceived in the early design phase, what it may look like, and – as we will see later – how it may behave. As I have pointed out before, we must see all objects, including the 'I' and individual building components, as actors, as active players in a parametric world. An actor is different from an object since it has an internal drive to act. Now what drives the cup to be a cup and to reside on the table? What drives the 'I' to put the cup on the table? What drives the table to hold the cup? What drives the coffee to stay inside the cup? And when we investigate further the characteristics of the materials, what components constitute the coffee and support it to be labelled as coffee? What happens in the exchange surface between the coffee and the cup? What forces impose the coffee on the cup? And vice versa, what forces impose the cup on the coffee? What are the forces from cup to table, from table to cup? Furthermore, what is the relation between the 'I' and the table, which functions as a destination for the cup as seen from the viewpoint of the 'I'? For the quick and dirty understanding of the subject of this book, I need to emphasize the importance of understanding the nature of the interacting components: I, cup, coffee and table. Parametric relationships must always be seen as bidirectional. There is always a balance between pushing and pulling, between being pushed and being pulled. There is a person, a fluid and some objects involved in this interactive scene, components of different kinds, and yet interacting. All interacting components have an impressive history behind them making them into what they are.

Now replace the 'I' by the designer, the cup by a vertical component (the component formerly known as the wall) and the table by a horizontally stretched component (the component formerly known as the floor), and we are talking architecture again. For the purpose of this book we need to first focus on the geometry of the components, scrutinizing their bilateral relationships on the level of geometry, and second, we need to focus on their behaviour, inserting the geometry and all actors in a serious design game, evolving in real time.

1.7 Feel the Force

A parametric relationship must be understood in terms of information exchange. The 'I' informs the cup to be placed on the table. The designer informs the bottom surface of component 1 to be connected to the top surface of component 2. To be able to design software for parametric structures it is crucial to make a complete functional description – a script, a scenario if you wish – of all commands that are set into action to relate component 1 to component 2. The two components need to share a point of reference, separately specified for each component. The points of reference are the active members of the point cloud. Once the points have been defined properly, one may connect the two points so that they share the same coordinates in an agreed-upon coordinate system. Once connected, the two components must calculate the area of contact they share. If the bottom part of a component is flat, it will be the full surface area of the standing part that is shared. This area will be used for the structural calculations, transferring the loads from standing to lying element. It is not my intention to technically describe what algorithms run in the parametric software to perform these basic calculations. Ultimately it is my intention to be empathic to the force fields between the components, to *feel* the forces while designing. Feeling the forces in an empathic and sympathetic way is the prerequisite to elevating the basic technique of parametric design to the level of behavioural design. One needs to internalize the forces. Information exchange from point to point, from surface to surface needs to be seen as streaming information, not just as an instance from a stream. Working with streaming information has an emotional effect on the behavioural designer. I will describe the emotions involved later on in the sections titled 'Flatland' and 'Spaceland'.

By streaming in both directions, both components inform each other continuously about their conditions. For example, when the standing component 1 has varying loads due to changing wind conditions, it needs to transfer the real time dynamic data in a streaming fashion to the supporting horizontally stretched component 2. Think of applying this dynamic concept to a one-mile-high building. Such a high building would sweep several metres to the left and right and cause nausea for users of the top floors. Now assume that we build into the load-bearing steel structure a series of actuators that actively resist changing wind forces, thus levelling out the influence of the winds. Then the one-mile-high structure will stand perfectly upright without any movement in the top. It will stand like a human does, balanced in the wind, stressing muscles to counter the wind. Such a structure would need to send updates in milliseconds to keep track of the changes, allowing the actuating components to respond and reconfigure accordingly.

006 CET BIM

CET IN OPENING WINDOW REVIT

_autodesk.com

In the summer of 2007 ONL won an international tender with project developer Porto to build a cultural/commercial centre in the heart of the Pest side of Budapest, on a unique location on the banks of the Danube. The nonstandard design includes the conversion of the old Közraktárak warehouses, and completes it with a bold new structure that juts out southward towards new developments along the river. By the end of 2010 the building will be finished. The design stands out as an uncompromising example of nonstandard design. The notion of nonstandard was promoted by a small but influential group of cultural elite in Budapest early in the twenty-first century who interviewed us for Atrium and Octogon magazines. There were also designs submitted by other players in the international arena, such as a kidney-shaped design by Zaha Hadid on Tervita Square and a design by Asymptote in the odd form of two giraffe heads. These projects stranded because of their financial and urban arrogance, the ignoring of urban rules and financial constraints. We did not fall into that trap. While respecting the urban guidelines and respecting the budget, we were able to complete the nonstandard design within these severe constraints.

One of the strengths of our successful formula was the Building Information Model (BIM) we modelled in Revit that allowed us to work in real time, connected with workgroups from both our Budapest and our Rotterdam offices. Eventually we were awarded the Autodesk Revit Experience Award in fall 2008, primarily because we were able to import our complex triangulated geometry into the otherwise somewhat rigid parametric software, and model the steel structure using wireframe mesh. One person in Budapest would control all concrete components, another the old warehouses, a third all installations, while the nonstandard geometry was controlled in Rotterdam. All groups made daily updates of their work to the workgroup. (Instant updating was possible in principle but would have taken too much transmitting time, and hence would have slowed down the work.) Autodesk was happy with the achievements, which made them decide to show the CET rendering in the opening window of Revit version 2010, and also on the cover of the Revit 2010 CD cassette.

007 AL NASSER HEADQUARTERS BIM

In 2006 ONL won an invited international competition for its design of the Al Nasser Headquarters tower in Abu Dhabi, United Arab Emirates. The client, Mr Al Nasser, owns a steel company and chose our design although it was, by far, the most challenging of the competition entries, as he liked the exposed nonstandard steel structure inside and the metal duotone finishing of the exterior façade panels. It wasn't until later that the client, represented by Northcroft Middle East, realized that all steel components and all windows are different in shape and dimensions. Al Nasser and Northcroft were both thrilled and suspicious of whether this would be feasible within the strictly commercial budget defined for this project. Thanks to the full control we had over the data as extracted from the Revit BIM model we were able to convince them that it was indeed feasible. Our BIM model has served many purposes. In the first place ONL dedicated one person, Gijs Joosen, to be both project architect and BIM modeller, so that no information was lost in translation. The BIM model allowed us to tweak the curvatures of the shape until the maximum gross floor area (GFA) was reached while maintaining the uniqueness of all constituent components and the unique amount of square metres for each floor. A change in the curvature would affect the quantum of square metres of each floor and hence the allowed GFA. Furthermore, it allowed us to communicate with high precision with the local architects, ACG, who were responsible for acquiring the building permit and for the calculations of the steel structure. The Al Nasser Headquarters tower is now under construction and will be finished in 2011.

1.8 From protoBIM to quantumBIM

The Building Information Model (BIM) allows 3d geometry to de-fine the wireframe, the surfaces and the volumes. The components are also labelled with properties and their performances described. Virtually everything that has geometry is organized in the BIM. The ideal BIM is a parametric model, meaning that each individual component has a strictly defined relation to its neighbouring com-ponents and to its object family. Changing one component means changing the local and global relations among all the components involved. Adding one component means creating new relationships. As relations are always bidirectional, both of the components are affected by the relationship. Explained in more prosaic language, the wall *stands* on the floor, while the floor *holds up* the wall. As all relations are subject to constraints, and, as we will point out later, in many BIM programs unnecessarily discriminative constraints, not all relations are possible. The main reason for this is that the BIM supporting programs are not written by designers but by techni-cians. They do not know better than to accept worn-out conventions from traditional design practice. The problem is in the agreed-upon existence of standard digital libraries. Once an object is labelled as a wall it can never become a door. Once you have chosen the family of floors, their members can never become walls. Once building components are defined as separate species in a building catalogue, they will only be allowed to have a limited number of relationships

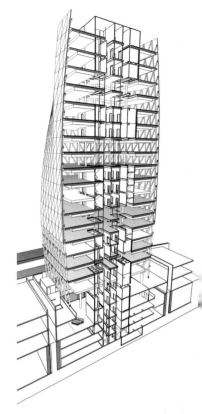

BIM AL NASSER HEAD- QUARTERS
_ONL [Oosterhuis_Lénárd] 2008

with other species. Similar to different species in nature; once a donkey, nevermore a horse, they simply can no longer crossbreed. When looking at the images of ONL's nonstandard architecture practice it is obvious that these traditional categories have become obsolete. A door becomes a specification of the homogeneous structural shell system. The door is not chosen from a catalogue of doors but rather is a further local specification of the structural system itself. According to this approach each designer will create a specific cellular system for a particular project in which the specifications of the originating cells signify specific tasks, for instance to be a door with hinges. But there is always a road back. One can always return to the cellular state where the moving part was not yet specified to move.

SWARM BEHAVIOUR OF POINT CLOUD IN .HRG SOFTWARE
_ONL [Oosterhuis_Lénárd] / Hyperbody 2005

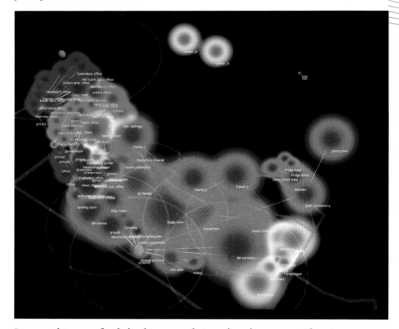

In searching to find the key to solving the above specification dilemma, Hyperbody has developed a program based on the dynamic principles of swarm behaviour. The Hyperbody Research Group software organizes the behaviour of points in space so that these points are provided with characteristics such as strength, area, volume, colour, shape. Positive strength means attraction, negative strength means repelling the points they are linked to. The swarming points are typically represented by vaguely outlined dots to avoid clinging to a specific aesthetic preference in these early design phases. Nonstandard information architects know that Platonic geometry cannot be the starting point for their designs. They must move deeper into the genes of the design materials. The relations between the points of the informed point clouds in digital weightless space give structure to the early design concept. The forces of gravity are introduced in a later stage to avoid the dominance of the ground level.

Hyperbody has teamed up with ONL to develop special software for such early design phases. It is common knowledge that the earliest conceptual design phase is the major driving force for any project. The very first design decision has a far bigger impact than all subsequent design decisions. The software that ONL/Hyperbody is in the process of developing, named protoBIM, supports development from a written conceptual statement via a swarming behavioural point cloud towards a BIM that contains all required data for building approval and the tender process. protoBIM connects all relevant disciplines to each other in this early design phase in the most effective and simplest fashion. The only data exchanged is that which is strictly necessary. Structural engineers do not need complete 3d models from the conceptual designer, rather they need to see a simple wireframe that they can import into their specialist calculation software, most likely applying finite element methods. protoBIM does not yet support streaming information, but this will be the main feature of a next level Hyperbody software that I call quantumBIM, which is protoBIM with features added to support streaming data at all data exchange levels based on the same principles of swarm behaviour. protoBIM communicates via a dynamic database with other programs, but only in quantumBIM will the cells of the database be continuously updated in a streaming fashion, feeding the actuating building components. quantumBIM is being prepared for the paradigm shift foreseen from static to dynamic modelling that will facilitate truly dynamic structures, addressed in real time and proactively acting in real time. protoBIM supports truly nonstandard architecture while quantumBIM facilitates truly dynamic structures.

1.9 One Building One Detail

One building, one detail. I have introduced this challenging phrase in earlier writings (paper for Nonstandard Praxis, MIT conference, 2004). With no reservation I declared 'Mies is too Much!' By radicalizing the minimalist tendency of Mies van der Rohe, I observed that Mies still needed many different details to prove his point that 'Less is More'. His Less is still Too Much. His Less is an imposed Less in visual appearance, but still a More in the number of details.

A better way is to have one single parametric detail mapped on all surfaces, subject to a range of parameters that render the values of the parametric system unique in each local instance, thus creating a visual richness and a variety that is virtually unmatched by any traditional building technique. This is the real More, based on the truly Less. Please be aware of the double meaning. I do respect Mies van der Rohe greatly, which I believe prohibits one to copy or vary from the original. So it was a deliberate violation when, in the early days of his career, Rem Koolhaas forced the Barcelona Pavilion to bend. A better approach would have been to radicalize Mies instead. The parametrization of the primary building detail implies an extreme unification; it requires an uncompromising systemic approach, thus allowing for a rich visual diversity at the same time. *Les extremes se touchent.*

The strategy to induce tension by introducing opposing poles, which will be further discussed in the 'Make That Body' section, is applicable to the design attitude towards generative detailing as well. Not only did I introduce opposing poles in master planning

(Manhal Oasis), in the body plan of building bodies (the Saltwater Pavilion, Space Xperience Center), but in the generic structure of the basic architectural detail as well. The parametric detail is generated just by executing a simple rule while retrieving local data for each individual node. Simplicity is thus intrinsically tied to multiplicity. Its intelligence is embedded in the swarm behaviour of the node, the programmable dot of the informed point cloud. I applied the above one-building, one-detail strategy to the design for the Web of North-Holland. The whole construct consist of one single but elaborate detail. All details including the two giant doors are members of one big family, described by one single script (Autolisp routine) mapped on the points of the point cloud as distributed on the doubly curved surface of the emotively styled volume.

1.10   *Just There, Just Then, Just That*

I say 'no' to columns, beams, doors and windows from a standard catalogue. Instead of making a tasteful selection from the building catalogue, instead of becoming a elitist connoisseur of high culture, I am in favour of designing and building project-specific build-ing components. So for every new building there would be a new consistent set of interlocking building components. It requires no further explanation to see that the giant door in the Web of North-Holland, which is basically a cut-out of the building body, is a door in the Web of North-Holland only; it cannot be applied in any other design. It belongs there, it does not fit anywhere else, it forms *that* intrinsic part of *that* design. Just there, just then, just that. It is the logical consequence of mass customization that an end product like a door from the standard catalogue will not fit anywhere in the body.

    In this context I must seriously criticize the buildings of Gehry. From a distance one would be tempted to see them as sculpture buildings, but at closer investigation they are not at all like that, for all Gehry's designs are based on traditional spatial planning, like arranging box-like spaces and wrapping them in the upper floor levels with a decomposed arrangement of loose fragments. Doors, windows, entrances are traditional as ever, based 100 per cent on the technology and aesthetics of mass production. There is noth-ing nonstandard about it. The same is true of many other build-ings designed by members of the deconstructivist Architectural Association gang from the 1980s – the Tschumis, the Coops, the OMAs; they all are trapped in their decon composted language. They have not been willing to loosen the strings to the traditional building industry as they have always relied on stylish catalogue products for the majority of their buildings' components. They still consider mass production as beautiful. Even when the exteriors of their designs use the metaphor of the nonstandard, their insides are full of column grids, beams, doors, walls and windows, all straight from the catalogue. They mistake the *complicated* for the *complex*. Decon designs are complicated indeed, they need a stack of dif-ferent details, while nonstandard architecture is complex, based on only one or a few different details, all members of a parametric family. Decon modernist building logic typically wastes resources, while nonstandard logic utilizes resources in a more efficient way.

Decon modernist style relies on mass production, nonstandard relies on industrial customization. The essence of the nonstandard is that each and every building component is precisely defined in the design stage, and then computer numerical control (CNC) produced. Each building component possesses a unique number to be addressed by the design and engineering scripts, hence, in principle, unique in its shape and dimensions.

1.11   *The Chicken and the Egg*

Which came first, the chicken or the egg? My answer is simple: the chicken and the egg are two instances of the same system, meaning that in each stage of development of the chicken-egg system there are both the chicken and the egg. Naturally neither the chicken nor the egg are worthy of that name in their early development phase, because they are not very specified in the earliest versions of the adaptive chicken-egg system. Chickens are something more like worms, and hard to distinguish from their eggs. I assume that self-copying and giving birth are equivalent events before the chicken-egg speciation process takes off. Similar to the chicken-egg problem there is a causality dilemma between nonstandard designs and computer numerical controlled (CNC) fabrication, the nonstandard design being the chicken; CNC, the egg. While the nonstandard design is fully controlled by a logically consistent parametric system describing precise positions, dimensions and geometry of each individual unique component, the execution process – in bio-lingo this may be referred to as the offspring – must follow the same logic. Exact parameters drive the design model, and the same exact values as extracted from the 3d BIM by means of automated procedures (Autolisp routine, scripting) must feed the production process. There must not be a quick and dirty translation, nor a remodelling, which always will turn out to be a reinterpretation, and there absolutely may not be any human intervention in the nature of the data as that is bound to be the cause of many inconsistencies and inaccuracies. Nothing may be lost in translation. The chicken can only produce and lay her own egg, the egg cannot be produced and assembled by another party applying another systemic logic. In the ONL Design and Build practice it was found that the occasional mistakes that occurred were always due to erratic human interventions in the file-to-factory process. Human interventions are bound to blur the consistency. The sloppy accuracy and emotional logic of human measuring or counting simply does not match up to the machine logic.

But don't worry, I am not trying to exclude people from the process. Humans do play the leading role in establishing the concept, in making intuitive choices from a vast multitude of possibilities, in declaring what is beautiful, in every aspect of the design and the building process where the communication with other human beings is crucial. But mind you, humans are not good at counting, not good at complex calculations, not good at the consistent application of procedures, not good at working overnight. People are always tempted to rethink a procedure while executing it, to rethink a process while running it, and typically to change the rules while playing. Also the brain is very slow in calculations, so much slower than the personal number cruncher, the PC. In order to catch up with the current societal complexity, an ever-expanding evolutionary process, the information architect has had to develop machinic extensions, exo-brains, exo-memories, exo-hands, exo-arms and exo-bodies to design and execute the nonstandard designs. That is why nonstandard design and file-to-factories production are two sides of the same coin. There could not exist a truly nonstandard design without CNC production; there cannot exist chickens without eggs, nor eggs without chickens.

PALAIS-QUARTIER FRANKFURT

_Massimiliano Fuksas /
photo Kas Oosterhuis

008 PALAIS QUARTIER FRANKFURT

One roof, one detail. But look carefully, the detail is welded with very low precision. There was the nonstandard conceptual design of Massimiliano Fuksas, there was the wireframe, but it was not executed as a nice 3d puzzle via a controlled CNC production process. The steel was manually drawn in 3d, not generated by scripts as it should have been. Many of the steel components were cut to length on site, and the pieces were welded together on site. I show this example for educational reasons, not to blame anyone in this project – not the architect, not the engineer, not the manufacturer. But it is obvious that something went wrong. The link between the file and the factory was obviously broken. There should have been an immediate link from a scripted high-precision detail to the high-precision CNC-produced components, to be dry assembled on site with zero tolerance, and definitely not welded on site since that introduces old-school imprecision. I experienced a similar problem while building the CET in Budapest.

Let me try to state the problem and suggest a solution. There can only be a correct solution if the problem is stated right. The problem is how to secure a sustainable nonstandard design and building process. The solution is to secure an unbroken link from BIM to CNC production to dry montage of the unique pieces of the 3d puzzle. Breaking the direct link, that is not transmitting the exact data from one phase into the next phase of the design and building process is a recipe for failure.

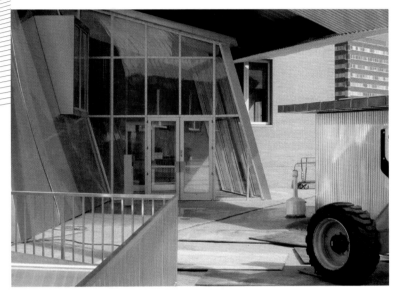

009 STATA CENTRE ENTRANCE

MIT STATA CENTER CAMBRIDGE
_Frank Gehry /
photo Kas Oosterhuis

As you slowly approach a Gehry building – any Gehry building from the Guggenheim Museum in Bilbao to the Stata Centre in Boston – the building appears more and more traditional. And when you finally enter the building, there is not much special about it. You enter through a regular façade, through regular doors, built up with regular profiles, in the deconstructivist way of using shapes brutally cut off at varying angles. Decon as usual, nothing nonstandard about it. We like Gehry Technologies for their great Digital Project software, but even Jim Glymph of Gehry Technologies told me back in 1998 that he freaked out when he saw some of our advanced achievements such as the design and execution of the Saltwater Pavilion at Neeltje Jans. Digital Project was created to rebuild Gehry's wrinkled and distorted silver paper models into something manageable and buildable. But when the starting point of the design concept remains rooted in old concepts, the realized building will communicate the outdated concept and not the new technology. There will always be an inconvenient friction between the design concept and the execution. It can be done, but it is not consistent, and it costs an irresponsibly large amount of money. Hence it is a threat to the consistent nonstandard designers who do strive for the unbroken links from generative design concept using parametric modelling in the earliest design phases to a proper CNC manufacturing.

1.12 *The New Role*
of the Nonstandard Architect

Every traditional intervention in the direct link from nonstandard design to CNC manufacturing will compromise the nature of the nonstandard design. Examples of such compromises can be seen in the making of the Water Cube and the Birds Nest for the 2008 Olympic Games in Beijing. And in my own practice I was subjected to a similar fate created by the predictably traditional attitude of the project developer of the CET project in Budapest. In all these cases the main contractor chose to weld the steel structure, compromising the accuracy of the structure by breaking the logical link from the complex geometry to an advantageous and consistent file-to-factory production of the skin. Once compromised, once the chain is broken, all future steps from there forward can no longer be re-linked to the CNC logic of mass customization. The process is killed, the egg does not lead to another life form, the umbilical cord is broken prematurely. Needless to say, each instance in which the logical chain is broken represents a major threat to the practice of nonstandard architecture, since the client may see only the blurred outcome and blame the inaccurate compromised details on the nature of the nonstandard design itself. But then again, can the contractors and the project developers be blamed for relying on their experience, which is largely based on traditional brick-and-mortar buildings? For them the nonstandard logic may not be logical at all; they are presumably not familiar with the advantages of the file-to-factory process since they are not using it. It is unknown territory for them.

Because of this reality nonstandard designers will need to rethink their contractual position as only consultants and will need to take on financial responsibility for the manufacturing process as well. When nonstandard architects such as I have full control and full confidence that their data are correct and accurate, they must take on the responsibility for the engineering of the geometry, and naturally must be paid proportionally for this responsibility. Since nonstandard architects are among the few parties to have a full knowledge of how the CNC production procedures are embedded as part of the logic of the design itself, they should be remunerated for taking the responsibility for managing the direct link from design to engineering as well. The benefits for the building industry will be huge: no more mistakes in the correctness and transfer of the data, no more delays in the exchange and understanding of the concept, no more need for remodelling, production will be clean and precise, assembly will always be correct, all steps in the design and building process will be just in time, and just what is needed. No more waste of time and materials as the building site will be clean, since recycling can be developed to cover all used materials.

There is one important condition though. All production must be computer numerical controlled, all components must be prefabricated, including all concrete structures, including the foundations. Now if I do all that, then I can be absolutely sure that I will perform twice as well, in other words a 100 per cent increase in efficiency, just by avoiding bureaucratic procedures, avoiding an abundance of building mistakes, avoiding the production of waste material, and in the process keeping the building site extremely clean. How sustainable can you get? It is obvious that the non-standard architect who controls the efficiency of the process must be the first to take profit from that expertise. The appropriate way to implement the new role of the architect is to have the architect have a financial stake in the building process. At present, architects leave the financial responsibility to the project developers and the contractors, so the architects act as consultants only, being responsible for no more than their designers' fee. I am advocating a new professional role for the architect, to become an entrepreneur by taking over the responsible role of the contractor for all components that are CNC produced. Architects are *chicken* if they do not have the guts to claim the leading role as the responsible designer-engineer-builder.

1.13 *Immediate Design and Engineering*

Not only should artists and architects work together from scratch, finding common ground and respecting each others' expertise, this applies to many other disciplines as well. One of the disciplines I am particularly keen on establishing immediate real time connections with is the discipline of structural engineering, as I consider structural engineers to be *designers*. Structural engineers should have an opinion on structures before negotiating with the architect designer. It is, however, necessary to rethink all aspects of design and reformulate all specific design tasks. There is a role for the concept designer, the form designer, the interaction designer, the structure designer, the climate designer, the exploitation designer, the user designer, the client designer, all of them designers in their own right. Basically they all are design nerds inhabiting their specific design niches. All stakeholding parties should establish one-to-one bidirectional relationships with each other, respecting their mutual expertise.

This does not mean that all people should sit in *en masse* during populated design sessions. On the contrary, I advocate one-to-one, peer-to-peer design sessions only. I do not see design sessions as a tedious collective effort at all, but as individual design efforts based on each designer's own specific expertise, immediately connected bi-directionally to the design niches of the others, all players in the design game performing to the best of their knowledge. I see the ideal evolution of the design process as a series of one-to-one speed dates, either physically or on the Internet, the progress of the work Web-based documented and available for all other stakeholders in a concurrent versioning system (CVS). CVS is a Web-based communication tool that software developers use for multiplayer open source development. My Hyperbody team has developed a tool named XiGraph (http://sourceforge.net/projects/xigraph/) for immediate exchange of expert ideas between a form designer and a structural designer. For the application programming interfaces, changes in form are recalculated in real time by the structural designer's software, then the expert data from the structural designer are fed immediately back into the form. Thus a lively dialogue arises and grows. Structural design is not only about optimization of a given form, because from the logic of structural design the structural designer may also have influence on the form as proposed by the form designer. The form designers will not limit themselves to simple shapes; they will become professional styling designers, for example, proposing sharp folds fading out into smoothly curved surfaces, striving for a continuity of the lines, integrating different components into a larger whole. And then they will send their modifications and refinements immediately back via the data hotlink to the structural designer who will recalculate the new form, thus seeing the effect of the styling intuitions immediately based on accurate calculations. All types of designers will try to maximize their sphere of influence, always exploring the overlap area where they can perform to the best of their abilities, allowing that overlap to grow bigger and bigger until there comes a moment when a critical mass is reached when the disciplines can be said to be fused.

My partner in life and business, Ilona Lénárd, who has trained as an actress and as a visual artist, and I have lived through that evolutionary process together. During the late 1980s and early 1990s, we worked on fusing art and architecture until both of us were happy with the results and were ready to launch the Sculpture City paradigm 'The Building Is a Sculpture, the Sculpture Is a Building' in 1994. Now the time has come to fuse design and *engineering* in all its aesthetic and technical aspects.

1.14 Immediate Design and Fabrication

Engineering is partly a consultancy task, partly a manufacturing task. ONL has participated in a Design and Build consortium that had the explicit goal of integrating the knowledge of the steel and glass manufacturers into the early design process for the projects Acoustic Barrier and Cockpit. Integrating the knowledge of the manufacturing process of industrial mass customization means knowing how the machines work, knowing what they can do. Mass customization is not about end products that are already on the market, like beams, columns, standard structural systems, geodesic dome structures or the like. Mass customization deals with informing a particular machine to produce unique products according the file-to-factory (F2F) process. The machines to which the ONL designs have been connected – in *idiot savant* style – are computer numerical controlled (CNC) machines that read sets of data. The integer data are provided by the designer engineer from ONL, and are straightforwardly used without any remodelling or rewriting for the CNC production. This means a tremendous increase in efficiency, and a total exclusion of building mistakes. Such a F2F script is either completely wrong; 'It doesn't work', or completely right, *'It works'*, and can be verified. This is as close as design can come to science. When it works correctly, all data are by definition integer and do not need to be reconstructed by an engineering consultant. Thus a direct link between designer and manufacturer is established.

This does not mean that the structural designer as a special consultant is no longer necessary in this process, not at all. In a fashion similar to that explained above, a direct link will be established, with the ultimate goal to establish the links in real time, between the concept designer and the structural designer and between the structural designer and the F2F designer. Always one-to-one, peer-to-peer (P2P). In the case of the Acoustic Barrier and the Cockpit, ONL established both the P2P connection between the form designer and the structural designer, and between the form designer and the F2F designer. The paradigm shift for collaborative design and engineering in real time is simply this: every player must be connected, preferably in real time, to each of the other players through a bilateral exchange of integer data.

**3D WEAVING
TEXTILE GROWTH
MONUMENT**
_Ilona Lénárd 2005

1.15 *Structure and Ornamentation*

Here now in the beginning of the twenty-first century there is a fascination for weaving in the architectural air. It is like a meme spreading all over from advanced private practices, then infecting students internationally, and from there affecting the large body of architectural practices. Early adopters developed design proposals applying three-dimensional weaving as early as a decade ago. Ilona Lénárd proposed a radical version of 3d weaving in her design for the Textile Growth Monument for the city of Tilburg in 2005. Now we see the fascination for weaving in many student projects, from the AA in London to Hyperbody at Delft University of Technology. Superficially speaking, it is just fashionable. But there is more, it has a deeper meaning, much more radical than just fashion. Three-dimensional weaving is appealing to that new approach in the international design practice where the design concept is deeply interlaced with structure and ornamentation. The fusion of the approach of the artist and that of the architect naturally leads to such an intertwining of disciplines and effects. If architecture and structure are merged successfully, such as in ONL's Cockpit in the Acoustic Barrier, then the specification of the details is bound to become equal to ornamentation. Not the obsolete kind of ornamentation added to an otherwise bare structure, not that empty wall waiting to be decorated, not that kind of ornamentation Adolf Loos was arguing against. The kind of ornamentation of today's nonstandard praxis is a further logical specification of the conceptual drive of the design. The kind of ornamentation I mean here is the refinement of the structural detail in all aspects of the building body.

When I look at the façade of the Al Nasser Headquarters in Abu Dhabi that I designed with my ONL team (and, as I write, is under construction and scheduled for completion in 2011), the varying pat-

COCKPIT

_ONL [Oosterhuis_Lénárd] 2005 /
photo Frank Hoekstra

52° 06' 46'' N
5° 02' 39'' E

tern of the windows, although fully functional and structural, communicates the idea of ornamentation. All of the 1,000 windows are different, directly derived from the logic of the tessellation of the ruled surfaces of the nonstandard design. It looks decorative, but it is also a pure logical specification of the chosen design approach, based on the manufacturing process of mass customization. The wide variety of window sizes within the same species feels like the variety of the leaves of a tree. Leaves that get more light grow bigger, leaves in the wind and/or in the shadow grow up in a harsher climate and hence remain smaller. This variety collects the first appraisal of being ornamental. Then if we direct our gaze towards the window bays we see more detailed features, and again, based on the uniqueness of the smaller components, it is pleasant to look at because of its lively variation. Rich specification and abundant variation of the architectural design take on the visual appeal of ornamentation, hence form and structure *includes* ornamentation.

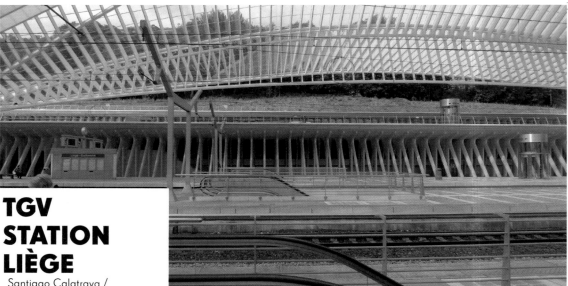

TGV STATION LIÈGE

_Santiago Calatrava /
photo Kas Oosterhuis

010 TGV STATION IN LIEGE SANTIAGO CALATRAVA

One day in spring 2010 we went to see Santiago Calatrava's TGV train station in Liege and Shigeru Ban's Centre Pompidou subsidiary in Metz. Although at first sight each applies similar technologies, the contrast between the two buildings could not be more dramatic. Both buildings cost a fortune, but were they worth it? I heard a Belgium architect declare that Calatrava is a bank robber, so expensive the building of the TGV station turned out to be. I have been there, I can see that it must have been expensive. But it is worth it, as in all its pores it communicates clarity and, consistency. I am convinced that this building will have a long life and will be respected as an inspiring insertion into the otherwise decayed city fabric of Liege. There is no doubt that Liege will benefit from it in the long run. The structure itself is a great example of the integration of design and structure, of visual lightness and structural performance. When one takes a pleasant stroll through it one sees that it is, without a doubt, based on functional logic – a structure that features large dimensions for the free-span roof and features delicate dimensioning and detailing for the shops and the cafés, where the public can literally feel the structure and the materials from which it is made. Being there makes one feel a part of an unfolding movie, as if one is an active player as are the movements of the trains, the comings and goings of the cars to and from the parking garage, as is the dynamic structure. The flow of people and the feature lines of the architecture merge in a convincing way. One cannot help but physically feel the real time motion interlaced with the frozen dynamics.

CENTRE POMPIDOU METZ
_Shigeru Ban /
photo Kas Oosterhuis

011 CENTRE POMPIDOU METZ SHIGERU BAN

From Liege we went on to Metz to see the new Centre Pompidou annexe designed by Shigeru Ban. Ban was chosen in an international competition, most likely on the basis of the sympathy of the jury for the roof structure. Unlike the roof of the TGV station by Calatrava, this roof has no spatial or structural connection to the structures placed on the ground floor level. Whereas Calatrava designed a spatial and structural continuity of roof and supporting structures on the lower levels used by the people, Ban has chosen an extreme disconnection between the wooden basketry roof and the stacked and rotated, contained rectangular boxes on the ground. The clash between the ground-based structures and the roof hurts my professional eye. There simply is a frozen conflict. On further inspection of the Centre Pompidou annexe we also encountered dozens of unresolved conflicts inside the disconnected structures themselves. The roof seems at first glance to be generated using generative components, but in reality it is a projection of a non-parametric repetitive system on a doubly curved surface. Thus it represents a true clash between old-school mass production and modern nonstandard algorithms. The Ban building lacks the integrity that makes the Calatrava building a consistent masterpiece. That is why the TGV station is a true building, and the Centre Pompidou annexe is just a roof. The jury did not make the right choice; their vision was probably blurred by the illusion of sustainability.

1.16 Flatland and Spaceland

From Flatland (*Flatland* by Edwin A. Abbott, 1884) to Spaceland is a huge leap from one dimension into another. Flatlanders are not equipped to notice spacelanders; they have no clue of the concept of space. They may see shadows of spacelanders, but have no idea where the shadows are coming from. They may think that they come from some super-flatlander, or they may construct fantasies about higher beings. This is, of course, how religion works, and we know that believing literally in constructed myths based on flat knowledge is a recipe for misunderstandings and eventually war. On the other hand, spacelanders can observe the flatlanders without any problem, and flatlanders can see linelanders, and linelanders can easily internalize the life of pointlanders. Spacelanders see all sorts of flat objects crawling alongside each other in Flatland, but never on top or below one another. They see the flatlanders move like cars on the motorway, like a pen on paper, like a computer mouse on the table, like plans and sections. The analogy between flatlanders and spacelanders is fully applicable to the world of architecture in the jump from straightforward plans and sections to complex geometry. Any architect who starts drawing a plan or a section while intending to design a space is doomed to be blind in Spaceland. That designer thinks and acts like a flatlander and acts as if living in Flatland while actually living in Spaceland. Wanting to design a space and then drawing plans and sections instead is equal to wilfully creating disinformation, and must be avoided at all times.

Unfortunately most design software makes it easy for the designer to start with plans and then extrude the surface along the vertical axis. As a design process this is so extremely poor that any designer should avoid this deadly trap and use the software in a more imaginative way. If one has no alternative to this poorly constructed computer-assisted design (CAD) software, then at least start with modelling volumes, parametric masses that can be tweaked, inflated and deflated locally and globally. Start with modelling a flexible ball as the first designer cell of the project. Make calculations of how many cubic metres the ball has, and make it subject to forces from the environment and from driving forces from within. Such a flexible ball can represent the originating cell, the informed mother cell that can be divided and specialized into more cells (rooms, spaces, membranes, atmospheres), eventually up to the highest level of detail, as hairs on the skin, as bolts in a steel structure. Or, start with a point cloud of reference points floating in endless space, and build your own universe of points. Establish behavioural relations between those points, as do the birds in a swarm. But never start with a plan or a section.

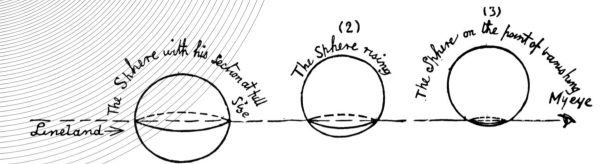

1.17 Inclusion and Exclusion

To start a design process with the plan and the section is an exclusive approach, which is why it is so poor. It excludes thousands of possibilities, and so the designer will never be able to consider these possibilities. The Flatland-based designer will never touch upon the rich world of complexity. The potential of nonstandard architecture will forever be unknown, out of reach, invisible. And when the unfortunate plan and section designers see a shadow of their world outside their world of plans and sections they will feel restless, and they will start behaving in a defensive way. At first they will try to deny the existence of the shadows and later will declare them to be a threat to their own small world. This is how traditional brick-and-mortar architects behave with respect to nonstandard architecture. They see the shadows of complexity, but they do not have a clue where they come from or what they mean. Therefore they at first deny their existence, they physically resist seeing them, and eventually they become hostile to nonstandard architecture. Poisoned by fear, they cannot do anything other than build a wall around their poorly informed planar world, protecting themselves from the alien, presumably of the dangerous kind. Think of the movie *The Blob* (1958), where the extremely mouldable alien, a soft but deadly toxic organism, is presented as the ultimate threat to mankind. This Blob could only be hammered by freezing it. But I know, and there are many of my peers who feel the same, that the alien is friendly and inclusive, and deserves a warm welcome. Flatlanders can become Spacelanders just by acquiring new essential skills, equivalent to learning a new language, or getting a pair of new exo-eyes, to provide for a sort of augmented reality, augmenting their flat world with an informative dimension. Then they will realize that the plan and the section are only paper-thin instances of the higher reality of complex volumetric forms described by nonstandard mathematics. The Flatlanders do not have to fear losing their old habitats since their plans and sections can still be properly described by their new space language. They can always organize nostalgic flat meetings and recall memories of times gone by.

**THE SPHERE
ENTERING
FLATLAND**
_Edwin A Abbott

The paradigm shift towards nonstandard 3d is inclusive, as nonstandard 3d includes all possible plans and sections and all possible volumes, including the pristine Platonic forms. Only a very specific parameter set will lead from the complex back to the planar, while all other parameters will generate visually complex and dynamic shapes. This does not at all mean that all possible forms are equally good or exciting. It takes a completely new professional attitude to learn to swim in the new deep space of nonstandard geometry. It takes years before one sees the difference between streamlined potatoes and stylish emotive building bodies. An illustrative example of a streamlined potato is the interior design of the restaurant of the Centre Pompidou, designed by Jacob McFarlane, a typical design exercise of beginners exploring the nonstandard paradigm.

ONL set their standards for nonstandard designs a decade earlier with the built emotive building bodies of the Garbagetransferstation (1994), the Saltwater Pavilion (1997), the Web of North-Holland (2002) and later the Cockpit in the 1.6-km stretched snake body of the Acoustic Barrier (2005). From the beginning I have realized the importance of style to be imposed on the *mouldable* complex shapes. Finally, a solid ten years after the very conception of liquid architecture, a 'lite' version of the nonstandard design attitude arrived in offices like Zaha Hadid and Asymptote. During the time in the early 1990s when I was busy defining the inclusive rules of nonstandard architecture, Hadid and the somewhat younger Rashid and Couture were still expressing themselves in the then dominant and retroactive deconstructivist language. Only after former students like Patrick Schumacher entered the profession did Hadid's work develop via dynamic fields theory and generative programming towards more or less nonstandard techniques and aesthetics. The majority of Hadid's recent proposals, however, are unlikely to be built, since they apply the aesthetics of the nonstandard language too superficially, not originating from a consistent internal nonstandard logic, thus putting her designs in the realm of capitalist bubble economy fantasy rather than placing them in a sound practice that is respectful of socially acceptable budgets. And what is worse, by plunging so decadently into the illusions of the global bubble economy, the potential of nonstandard architecture at large becomes compromised, making it more difficult to convince clients of the integrity, effectiveness and efficiency of consistent nonstandard designs. Therefore I can only conclude that Hadid compromises the potential and the intrinsic promise of the nonstandard, as related to CNC mass customization, to improve the general quality of the built environment and thus of the quality of life.

1.18 *The Nonstandard Includes Any Standard*

Nonstandard architecture (NSA) is inclusive in its very nature. The doubly curved surfaces (nurbs) of NSA are controlled by curves, and these controlling curves (Bezier curves) are in turn controlled by a series of control points, each with a set of parametric handles. By setting the parameters the designer can decide on the level of smoothness of the design. Imagine a nonstandard design with thousands of informed control points. Whereas a standard traditional planar design typically needs no more than a few dozen control points (with a minimum of eight points) to define a square volume, adding information to the straight lines by inserting control points informed by parameters renders them into informed curves. Setting the parameters back to zero recaptures the cubic volume, when the control points are still in place. This brief thought exercise shows clearly that the nonstandard approach includes standard prismatic shapes. The opposite is not true; prismatic shapes cannot describe a curved shape properly, which makes the nonstandard approach simply superior to the standard. Standard geometry is Flatland; nonstandard geometry represents Spaceland. Nonstandard geometry is one level higher in relation to Platonic geometry, representing a higher level of information. Software that is developed today by the commercial market should acknowledge this higher level of information. The software must support a building information model (BIM) capable of describing nonstandard geometry without any restrictions. As I write, only a few software packages (General Components, or GC and Digital Project, or DP) support complex parametric geometry properly, but regrettably these packages are based on proprietary software architecture, and so are not open source and not readily available to all participants in the design process. Therefore without an easy link to other less well-equipped design stakeholders, the process is bound to lose essential information in the process of bilateral data exchange. GC and DP are also simply too expensive for beginners in the NSA. Following the earlier described protoBIM strategy, the data exchange between the different disciplines and thus between the different software packages must be limited to the exchange of essential data, and using exclusively open source languages. The leap from proto-BIM to quantumBIM must be made when the design subject is a programmable structure, where the support of streaming data is mandatory. While quantumBIM is a vision for the near future, the protoBIM strategy can be implemented right away, needing just a mental switch. The technology is available, one only needs to educate oneself and jump into the deep end.

1.19 *Multicellular Bodies*

Now I need to discuss yet another design strategy. I need to look beyond monocoque structures, beyond single-celled volumes, that is, beyond the Waterpavilion, beyond the iWEB, beyond the Cockpit. Imagine three-dimensional structures, imagine multicellular volumes. Architecture at large is concerned with the spatial layout of multicellular bodies in time, with the membranes of the cells open, closed or semipermeable to a mix of air, liquid and information packages carried by infrastructure and people. The road forward towards a new kind of building is bound to be a road towards complex multicellular and adaptive bodies. On the way towards this new kind of building two major new paradigms must be adopted. First there must be a paradigm shift towards nonstandard geometry and subsequently a second paradigm shift towards real time behaviour. Like most other nonstandard practices, I first practiced nonstandard geometry via rather basic simple forms in monocoque structures, in analogy with car bodies and other product bodies. This was a logical starting place for me, since I am heavily inspired by product bodies, by product life, which represent to me the new clothes of nature. It is important to acknowledge that the actual state of the art of nonstandard designs is not an end game to complete all architectural development; it is just a first step towards an architecture of intelligent adaptive and proactive bodies.

Thus the logical follow-up step I have explored in recent years is the step towards the design paradigm of multicellular building bodies, based on three-dimensional Voronoi structures. Think of soap bubbles expanding in space, expanding towards their boundaries. You may wonder why soap bubbles are not rectangular. Actually, they would be rectangular if all forces working on them and working inside them had the same simple values for their parameters. And if the parameters driving the shape of the cells were indeed all the same, the soap bubble structure would look like the familiar multicellular three-dimensional gridded building. From evolution, however, we've learned that the forces from without and within the body are never evenly distributed since there are always subtle differences that eventually cause explicit variations in the spatial layout.

Currently I have reached the point of employing the mathematics of 3d Voronoi and digital scripting tools to explore the richness of difference, variation and speciation. Voronoi diagrams are named after the Russian mathematician Georgy Voronoi (1868-1908). Voronoi nodes are the points equidistant to three or more neighbouring sites. We applied the 3d Voronoi logic to the design for the Digital Pavilion in Seoul and to the design for the floating water pavilion in Yeosu, both in South Korea. Voronoi allows the designer to connect the point cloud of reference points of a programme of requirements to the conceptual spatial layout. The programme of requirements is vitalized and quantified with volumetric dots, each dot with its own absolute volume and its negotiated distance from neighbouring dots. The architectural appearance of the 3d layout is subject to manipulation of *top-down* imposed parameters to suit conceptual ideas, whereas the 3d Voronoi logic serves as the inner logic to describe the rules of swarm behaviour. It is not hard to imagine that when the positions of the point cloud are manipulated in such a way that the reference points are organized in a strict rectangular grid, the result of the 3d Voronoi calculation will be a rectangular multicellular structure. Thus multicellular Voronoi includes the traditional rectangular organization of gridded structures, yet at the same time offers much more than that by stimulating the richness of millions of possible spatial layouts. It is up to information architects to find their own personal style when exploring these millions of possibilities. Each time a new technology becomes available the designer must dive into the new deep end and learn to swim again.

2.

> *Shape That Body*

the point cloud is organized by powerlines to shape the body

012 RENAULT DEZIR BY LAURENS VAN DEN ACKER

Analysing concept cars is nearly a daily routine for my staff and me. A number of concept cars are developed for each car show to show the public, to test new directions, to inform the peer designers from other brands and are a testing ground for future production cars. There is an interesting current development in the relationship between concept cars and production models. The time gap between the concept car and the production model keeps getting narrower and narrower. Thanks to advanced computational tools in the design process and CNC machines in the manufacturing process of the prototypes, new concept cars can come more quickly to the market. There is a clear tendency towards an almost immediate production of a series of fully functional prototypes. The ultimate step would be production on command, as we already are familiar with printing on demand. In earlier days this was a privilege of the rich, but ICT in design and manufacturing makes the uniqueness of a special design available to a larger public.

I am always interested to see what features are considered in the design of concept cars. For example, the seating concept of the Renault DeZir interior reminds me of our Web of North-Holland pavilion, where we kept the spaces between the Hylite aluminium panels (which are used in the automotive industry) open so as to allow a red lava-like glow to shine from the inside towards the outside, evoking a magical effect at night. The disciplines of car body design and architectural body design look at each other, learn from each other, and crossbreed.

RENAULT DEZIR
_carbodydesign.com

013 BMW GINA BY CHRIS BANGLE

The release of the prototype of the BMW GINA sports car occurred in 2009, almost a decade after car body designer Chris Bangle actually created it with his team at BMW. Why did they keep it a secret for so long? By analysing the GINA it is obvious that it served as a test case for the sharp feature lines that characterize the BMW Z4 sports car and which can be traced back to the BMW 1.3 and 5 series manufactured in the first decade of this century. But that is not why it was kept undercover. The real reason must be that this prototype was a bold exercise in emotional design, since the feature lines, as in the flanks, in the hood, surrounding the headlights, the seats, are programmable so as to change their curvature, and thereupon change their emotional value. Such had not been seen before in car body design. Yet it resonates completely with our approach towards a programmable architecture, as I introduced in the concept of a programmable building, Trans-Ports, in 1999 at the first Archilab Conference in Orléans. I used exactly the same reasoning as Chris Bangle did when developing his prototype. Both of us emphasized the embedded emotional values that can be addressed by instructing the actuators that are part of the very structural frame of the body. Both of us found out simultaneously, not aware of the endeavours of the other, that there is a strong emotional potential in the direct link between concept and computation. It is quite significant that my inaugural speech at Delft University of Technology (2001) was titled Towards an E-motive Architecture. Convergent evolution at work.

BMW GINA
_carbodydesign.com

2.1 The Concept Rules

The design concept deserves a crucial place in any profession. The concept represents a spark, an intuition, something that has not been out there before, often a new combination of known ideas that suddenly crystallizes in the mind of the designer, a singularity that appears in the architectural practice for the first time. The first conceptual idea represents the first and most important rule of a design process; the first rule dominates all other subsequent rules. The first conceptual idea determines in what direction the design process will go; the chosen first idea rules out all other possible first ideas. The concept is the first written sentence of the design script. As an example of how extremely top-down the nature of a design concept is, I'll use the design concept for ONL's new office in the existing sound barrier in Nesselande in Rotterdam. My design concept, simply put, is to replace a part of the acoustic dike with a 1000-m² building. The concept can be narrowed down to one single line of written script: *replace a part of the dike with a building*. This single sentence contains so much top-down information that as a first rule it eliminates billions of other possibilities that could be feasible on that site. The main function of a design concept is to narrow down possibilities, to give a specific non-negotiable direction to the future design effort, to choose a direction in a vast sea of possibilities. Choosing such a direction is an immediate and intuitive act, a sudden shortcut in the brain, a challenging fresh new combination of thoughts. After having stated the first conceptual idea, it must be quantified as soon as possible in order to start the subsequent design process, and in order to be able to communicate it to other players in the design game.

Any conceptual idea is related in some way to a shape with a specific geometry. This idea of replacing a part of the dike presupposes a *shape* of that dike. The shape of the dike thus forms a set of serious constraints for the building to be designed. These constraints limit the number of possible shapes of the scheduled building. Taking the first conceptual sentence literally, it means that the building will not stick out, that it will not be rectangular, that it will not bulge out, that it will not have a double curved surface, since the existing shape of the dike rules over every design decision that follows, otherwise it would not be replacing but redesigning. Thus, choosing the right words for the design concept is of major importance. But there is more, and it is even more important. This first line of script must be quantified. It is my observation from my practice that when designers accept the delamination of quality and quantity they lose control of their own design concepts. Thus a simple and straightforward initial conceptual sentence, when exactly quantified in a spreadsheet or table, will control top-down all further design decisions. It takes only four words (replace, part, dike, building) in a specified algorithmic relationship to narrow down all possibilities to only a few design options. The more a concept restricts further possibilities, the more likely that it is a recognizable, exciting, challenging, appealing and innovative concept. The art of conceptual design means first conceiving of a challenging bold concept and then making every effort to keep the initial excitement alive, avoiding deviation from the power of the initial conceptual idea. The basic rule is that the fewer words and numerical data one needs to describe the design concept, the more likely it is a powerful concept, where power is defined as a strong magnet serving as an attraction point placed somewhere in the future. These magnetic points attract the energy of a crowd of people such as clients, experts, manufacturers, managers, all of whom subordinate themselves to the power of the magnet and are voluntarily willing to synchronize their efforts to move into that direction. This is the power of the concept – the concept shapes things to come, the concept rules.

REPLACE A PART OF THE DIKE BY A BUILDING
_ONL [Oosterhuis_Lénárd] 2010

2.2 The Direct Link from Concept to Computation

The initial design concept is directly related to the shape things may take. In the case of the building replacing part of the dike, the shape can be described by simple geometry. Introducing geometry means introducing computation. Thus in the first conceptual idea the written word is directly linked to computation. The dike has a given dimension, the dike has a certain angle, the dike is built of certain materials with specific quantitative characteristics, the dike absorbs a given amount of decibels. When replacing a part of that dike, one knows where that dike is in the national system of coordinates, which gives an enormous amount of data and hence computation to the original conceptual idea. Then there is the weather, the water level, the prevailing winds. There is the number of decibels that must be absorbed by the dike. To put it in a different way, the concept has an environmental context with a mountain of data to connect to. I am convinced that it is important to build this connection to environmental data from the very beginning of the design process. Some values are fixed, like the angle of the slope of the dike, other values are parameters that can change according to the changing number of square metres required. In this stage of the design the assumed building is not yet anything other than a mouldable soft single-celled volume, with clear geometrical constraints as dictated by the shape of the dike. This cell can be stretched parametrically along the axis of the dike. Now connect environmental data to that cell. Three surfaces of the cell are facing the dike itself, while the three other surfaces are facing the open skies – one facing south, one facing up, one facing north, so this single-celled model must be linked to sun diagrams to monitor the sun radiation. The wind forces that push and pull the surfaces can be applied to the protoBIM. These basic calculations are top priority for the development of any design scheme in order to facilitate collaboration with other experts from the very beginning of the design process. When modelled properly, the amount of cubic metres of that single cellular space will be known and can be tweaked parametrically. Then the material performances for the enveloping surfaces of the originating mother cell can be chosen. One must set up the values parametrically using, for example, Rhino or Grasshopper, in order to be able to play freely with the values, in order to vary them endlessly, preferably using user-friendly sliders for setting the values. This allows the designer to act intuitively in this early stage, allows the designer to spend precious quality time on design issues instead of being inhibited by technical hurdles. I know this sounds like a paradox, but we must indeed link the design model to real time computation first before we can create the working space to act intuitively.

This is how it works. I need exact science and logic to free myself from conventions and to ensure that I can act intuitively. The technique must be built parametrically in such a way that whatever the designer chooses, all relations will be kept intact, with no mistakes possible, nothing forgotten, nothing lost in translation, no need to change because of unexpected values coming later from engineers. It is unfortunate that in daily practice important data often do come in later, too late, and require a complete remodelling of the design concept and often requiring a complete reformulation of the concept. The essence and the power of the original concept may be easily lost. Essential engineering must play an active role in the conceptual design procedure, which requires the direct link from concept to computational data. Many subsequent steps using parametric sliders correlated to the further development of the single-celled volume will follow. The design will be specified in greater detail, the single cell will split into more cells, like a fertilized cell dividing and specifying into functional subgroups, always keeping the relations with exterior and interior value drivers intact, and always able to be modified parametrically.

2.3 Multiplicity

Suppose that the concept to *replace part of the dike with a building* had been a concept to *build a building next to the dike*. No one would have been intrigued, it would have been regarded as business as usual, though it might still have become a great building. The excitement comes from the fusion of two separate unrelated entities: dike and building. Simply assuming that they will be deeply related brings about the excitement. This had not been seen as possible before, since it is almost as unlikely as the broken pieces of a cup falling upward into an undivided whole again. Fusion design brings unrelated objects together in an unprecedented way. The dike building design concept represents the principle of multiple usage of the ground, whereas the dike acts as a sound barrier, but is unmistakably a functional building as well, hitting two flies with one stroke.

The sustainable aspect of my design approach is to fuse different entities into a new more complex entity, comparable to the evolutionary jump from single-celled body to a two-celled body, *the chicken plus the egg*. While each cell had its own logic, the new two-celled body has augmented logic, more complex, in a stage leading to further specifications into even more complex bodies containing thousands of cells, a swarm of smaller ones (building components) and bigger ones (spaces), leading to a multiplicity of arguments, functions and material characteristics fused together in one single complex building body. The choice of fusion and multiplicity opens up new horizons, breaks down mental barriers, creates new species of building bodies, and eventually leads towards the self-proclaimed new kind of building.

2.4 Upstream

What is typical for a design concept, and for the dike building concept in particular, is that it is a problem-solving process without first having a problem. A problem-solving concept works its way upstream against the Second Law of Thermodynamics, which states that all energy tends to break down to a lower state of energy. Entropy is a measure of how organized or disorganized a system is. A higher level of entropy means less information and hence more disorder. Our universe tends towards higher entropy levels under normal circumstances. Proposing a concept is something special, a concept adds information to a local part of the universe. The design concept functions as an alien source that adds information locally. A concept functions as a magnet positioned somewhere in the future towards which all attention is directed, adding information to the system, and having the effect of locally lowering the entropy level. Unfortunately the entropy level is, in the world of science, defined such that a lower level of information or decreased order means higher entropy or more disorder. But let us look at it from the bright side. Design concepts travel upstream, decreasing the entropy level, increasing the body mass of information. Upstream thinking and acting extracts energy from its environment. Any upstream design concept means adding information, which goes hand-in-hand with a downstream loss of information. Adding information brings objects alive. Living beings are highly informed structures. Any strong problem-solving concept has a polarizing effect on the environment, it monopolizes information, it creates an information gap between the well informed and the poorly informed, hence it feeds on its environment. It is not a question of good or bad. It is an inescapable consequence of evolution that adding information endlessly will eventually lead to a world made of pure information. Of course this is a speculative thought, though a logical one. It justifies striving for a well-informed architecture with higher intelligence, with more robotics, more parametrics, more responsiveness, more adaptivity, more real time behaviour, more proactivity, feeding on its immediate environment by extracting ordered information from it, and thus, interestingly enough, making its immediate environment a little bit dumber. It is worthwhile to design better-informed objects, to strive for a meaningful complexity, which will surely be appreciated by a larger public. Better-

**COCKPIT IN
ACOUSTIC BARRIER**
_ONL [Oosterhuis_Lénárd] 2005

informed buildings will become appreciated as living structures, the public will care for them more than for static structures because they will experience them as *alive*. The public would rather watch a living bird than a stuffed specimen of a dead bird. The more the built environment proposes an intelligent dialogue with the users, ranging from extremely silent and frozen to talkative and excited, the more the public will like it.

2.5 Not a Fixed Recipe

For each new project I typically invent new design rules and new design tools. There is not a fixed recipe for all projects, there is only one specific procedure for one specific project, thus design strategies are typically project specific. I learn from earlier projects and cross-fertilize with project strategies from other architects, but I never repeat the same conceptual phrase. I do not mass-produce a series of the same designs, instead, designs are always customized to a certain site, time, budget and reason. Designs are just that, just then, just there, and above all just *thus*. Design concepts are by definition subject to evolution. Repeating the same concept is not really possible since the environment around the designer changes constantly, the available technology evolves at an ever faster speed, and the political opportunism of the public swings back and forth like a pendulum. Repetition of the same concept is a dangerous illusion. Repeating the same concept must be regarded as backward thinking, caused by a disillusioned retroactive mind. If a designer could only wait long enough to come up with the repeated design scheme, it would stand out as something completely nostalgic, something from older days, something from another culture, like a poor copy of a dusty museum piece. So design rules evolve with the unfolding times. However, this does not mean that all new design rules are strong and exciting, far from that. The majority of applied design rules are completely boring, blindly following trends, and result in weak copies of the stronger designs that the trend followers probably saw in a magazine. The quality of design concepts follows the logical distribution of the Bell curve, just as do many other aspects of life. The majority of design concepts are mediocre, while at the ends of the Bell curve there are the specials, especially weak and especially strong. Newness is an intrinsic aspect of evolution. When claiming to propose something new, I simply confirm that I am catching up with evolution. There is no way out of the evolutionary here and now, we are living inside evolution. And there is nothing more fascinating to me than that.

FLYOTEL DUBAI

_ONL [Oosterhuis_Lénárd] /
Mahmoudieh 2005

014 FLYOTEL DUBAI

The design concept for the Flyotel in Dubai is to celebrate the fascinaThe design concept for the Flyotel in Dubai was to celebrate the fascination for flying, although other conceptual and strategic thoughts crossed our minds as well. The idea was born during a conference in Shanghai where we met interior designer Yasmine Mahmoudieh and where we decided to enter the Dubai market in a joint effort with an iconic design for a hotel project. We designed the exterior; she designed the interior finishings. We presented the concept to a number of selected project developers and got an enthusiastic reception for our ideas, but even for Dubai this concept seemed a bit extreme. Nakheel was not sure whether they could build it; there were many unknowns for them. We knew we could do it because we had gained expertise with the nonstandard logic and we knew that it was at least as feasible as other projects being built in the Emirates. The Flyotel design is a demanding sculpture, 160 m high, the shape and skin based on the emotive design principles developed earlier, and now made possible by the currently available technology of industrial customization and taking advantage of CNC manufacturing techniques. The Flyotel houses a harbour for seaplanes arched by a conference centre and connected to the uprising sector of the body that is purposefully shaped like an elegant swan, illustrating the desire to fly and the ability to float. In the emotive styling of the body parts we introduced the feature of the narrow neck between the two major parts of the body, the hotel tower and the conference centre, both imagined to be floating on the water.

**U2 TOWER
DUBLIN 2003**
_ONL [Oosterhuis_Lénárd]

015 U2 TOWER DUBLIN

*The winning design for the U2 tower international competition was
an ordinary but twisted lighthouse, retro-styled to communicate, perhaps, that U2 is a light from the past. We chose a more exciting conceptual approach, placing the studio for the U2 band in a dualistic
setting with an open people's studio, as two poles of the same tension
field. Our concept should be seen as a declaration that U2 may think
they are King and on top of the world, but that they should always remember the fact that they are secondary to other bands, who are not
famous or not yet famous, but still make high-quality music. We orchestrated a lively dialogue between the two studios, to be linked by
a luminous layer of 'strange substance', as we labelled it. The strange
substance is a programmable structure that can change shape and
content in real time, one of the first applications of the concept of a
programmable structure, after the launch of our dynamic Trans-Ports
concept in 1999. The strange substance would move with the vibes of
music, set in motion by the actuating electric pistons in the glazed
structure, and the substance would change colours according to the
pitch of the score. We imagined a constant fight between the two
sides, fighting to change the colours, fighting for the right to mobi-
lize the strange substance. Only after having designed the U2 tower
did we realize that the shape of our competition entry captured the
force of a strong muscular arm in a bent position, as if to capture the
power of the U2 songs.*

**FSIDE
HOUSING
AMSTERDAM**
_ONL [Oosterhuis_Lénárd] 2008
/ photo Kas Oosterhuis

**52° 19' 10'' N
4° 57' 28'' E**

2.6 Opinion on the Curve

Strong design rules display a solid intrinsic logic; they are explicit and crystal clear in their definition. Strong design rules can be either of a top-down imposing nature or of a bottom-up generative nature. The rules must be radicalized in order to be described in a few clear lines of code. Textual prosaic code to start with, then lines of code in a software programming language as an immediate mandatory transcript. Design rules that cannot be clearly described and exactly quantified in a computer program are useless, one cannot work with them in a digital environment. Meaning that if one thinks one has a strong design rule, but that rule cannot be quantified, that one has a problem. Then the design rule is not a rule but a vague subjective idea, open to multiple interpretations, and hence a recipe for subsequent confusion. Then every stakeholder in the design process would make their own interpretations of the rule, and the design process would be compromised by conflicting mindsets, evidently counterproductive for a smooth design process. Let me give an example from practice. When I say that the building body will have a smooth curvature, I will need to define the nature of the curve. There are virtually unlimited types of curves, so I need to define a mathematically exact definition of my curve. I must have an opinion on the curve. Without a clear opinion on curves one would be doomed to descend towards a repertoire of infantile Barbapapa shapes. It must be clear by now that this is what I clearly reject. Defining the type of curve means setting the number of control points and the parameters for the control points, quantifying the number of points, quantifying the value of the parameters. The essence of any verifiable design act is to have an *opinion* on the applied geometry. The more specified your opinion is, the better you can communicate your opinion to other players in the collaborative design game, the better you can represent your ideas in an exchangeable digital format, thus excluding vagueness and confusion, therefore effective and efficient, gaining valuable design time and excluding future building mistakes.

2.7 Radicalize the Concept

Having created the initial conceptual idea, any designer will be quickly distracted by vague assumptions to compromise the validity of the concept. The concept will be subjected to a variety of arguments against it. It will be tested to check its fitness in a series of checks and balances. After the split-second concept passes the first test is when the really hard part of the design process begins. Serious doubts will start to creep into the design process and an army of forces will aim to destroy the concept. The art of retaining the power of a concept is to find ways to enhance the initial power with subsequent second- and third-order design decisions. While destroying a concept is fast and easy to do, the long-term nurturing of its character to its full strength until it is built is a complex task that requires perseverance and persuasiveness from the concept designer. My ecology professor used to say that war is fast and easy, while peace is slow and complex. Only truly strong concepts survive, that is, concepts that can stand up against multiple critical attacks.

The concept for the Cockpit in the Acoustic Barrier along the A2 motorway near Utrecht withstood many such attacks, but proved to be steadfast in changing circumstances, retained its purity, became an attractor for future clients, and gained even more power in the innovative process of nonstandard design and file-to-factory CNC manufacturing. Now the Cockpit has become a role model for integrating a building into an acoustic barrier along motorways. The lesson here is that the concept will need to be taken to its radical pureness in order to survive the inevitable attacks. Radicalized features are crucial in the process of natural selection. My strategy to survive is to not deviate from the intuitively chosen direction, not to change the subject, not to propose something different along the way, since all of that will confuse the client, and will cause the client to doubt that it is such a good idea after all. The best strategy is to radicalize the concept, to develop the first conceptual image to the extreme, without compromise. Only when an innovative concept is highly radical will it open the eyes of the client and be subsequently respected. Only then will the other stakeholders in the design process become excited, only then will something special happen, something that will be meaningful for a long period of time after that first split second of combinatory conceptual intuition. The power of a strong design concept is that it opens up new horizons and breaks down mental barriers, piling up credibility and paving the road to execution.

2.8 Powerlines

Existing software programs do not support intuitive design ideas, neither do they support immediacy in the design process. The interfaces of existing software programs are as of yet in an immature stage of development; they are much too technocratic. Existing software programs are usually built from the subsidiary point of view of draftsmen, not from the 'pushing the envelope' point of view of the speculating designer. On one hand I support the need for precision and exactness because I know this is the only way to develop proper communication via building information models with the other stakeholders in the design game. On the other hand I support the equally important force in the design process that facilitates the designer to be intuitive, to speculate fast and act impulsively in unknown territories. To support my intuitive side I might need to use existing software in a fashion that was not intended by the software developer, in the way Ilona Lénárd uses existing CAD software to sketch intuitively in 3d, bypassing the pre-set ideas of how to use the software. The inherent quality of every computation device is that even impulsive intuitive sketches, executed by hand gestures using the 3d digitizer or the 3d mouse, are precisely described mathematically and hence exactly quantified.

Ilona Lénárd refers to her fast and intuitive sketches as powerlines, gestures that are loaded with power. She typically has periods where she draws hundreds of quick sketches per day, with one particular sketch lasting no more than one or two seconds. There is no time for deliberation, the only way is to follow pure intuition. Her vision on powerlines is a personal opinion on the curve. Her gestures are curves by definition, since the gestures are made by arm and hand movements, moving with five degrees of freedom in wrist and shoulder, while the intention with which she moves the hand and arm represents her opinion on the curve. Projects like the Hydra inside the Saltwater Pavilion (1997) and the Wedding Chapel in Nanjing, China (2007) are literal translations of Lénárd´s three-dimensional intuitive sketches into a built structure. The art works of Lénárd show clearly that there is a potential for the design culture when exploring one's own intuition, and relating the intuitive emotionally laden gestures to exact computation. Intuitive sketches are fast and computation is fast, much faster than deliberate thinking by the human brain.

Lénárd has explored the principles of intuitive sketching using the 3d digitizer to link directly from gesture to computation. The direct link between intuition and calculation feels similar to the way an intelligent autistic person has direct access to the numbers in the telephone book. The mouse of the computer has only two degrees of freedom, limited as the mouse is to its own little flatland. Not only artists, but also modern information architects want to move more freely and break out of the limitations of the mouse pad. There is an urgent need for improved interfaces between the designer and the computing device to facilitate more natural bodily movement in the transfer of ideas from the imagination and intuition to the digital realm.

2.9 Project-Specific Design Tool protoPLAN

Suppose the existing software does not allow for the unintended use by the designer. In that case the designer must consider designing a customized design tool. This is what my ONL team and I have done for the Manhal Oasis master plan for the Manhal Palace site in Abu Dhabi, and for the Digital Pavilion project in Seoul. I asked my Hyperbody team of researchers to write a design tool for associative urban planning. The customized protoPLAN design tool for the Manhal Oasis master plan is grounded on the principles of swarm behaviour. The protoPLAN design basically is a serious game, where the designer acts while being a player in the game, acting inside the evolving design game itself. At the start of the design game one sets the overall Floor Area Ratio (FAR). Whatever spatial layout one is modifying, splitting, copying, moving or otherwise changing, that FAR is kept intact as the choice for the FAR rules over all other choices. The FAR is defined as a global constraint acting as an external force upon the parametric system, like the chess player acts on the chess board while respecting the internal rules of the game. Respecting the FAR is solely a density issue, not related to detailed styling issues.

One starts the game by compiling the whole amount of required square metres, 2,000,000 m^2 in the Manhal case, into one compact volume – the mother cell. One can manipulate this single cell entity to spread out evenly over the whole site by increasing the

**MANHAL OASIS
protoPLAN
DESIGN TOOL**
_ONL [Oosterhuis_Lénárd] 2006
/ Hyperbody Tomasz Jaskiewicz

projected area while retaining its single-celled nature. Further
specifications of the originating mother cell by splitting it into
many children cells forms the basis for further design choices.
Thus the division game unfolds. First I split the primary mother
body cell into four specified cells, one on either side of the oblong
playing field, currently the deserted palace grounds of the local
ruling family right in the centre of Abu Dhabi. The long sides are
subsequently split into a series of towers, the short sides into two
distinct functional groups, one commercial body cell at one end of
the site, and one cultural body cell along the central Airport Road
on the other side. The specification design game continues until
the desired resolution, positions, sizes, mutual relations and specific functions are identified. Independent of how many bottom-
up splits and fusions one makes, the FAR remains the same.
Specification is bottom-up from the inside out, FAR is top-down
from the outside in. The same is true for the bilateral relations
built between the split cells. For example, each tower is elasti-
cally connected with an educational module. When that tower is
moved, the educational module moves with it. In this way the local
relations are kept intact while respecting the global constraints.
As there is no commercial software performing like this, we had
to write the software ourselves, using the game development
software Virtools as the appropriate platform. Thus the design
process becomes a custom-designed design game played by the
stakeholders in real time.

2.10 Top-Down, Bottom-Up

Architecture is a balancing act between top-down pressure and
bottom-up release. Personally I prefer these two forces that work
on the design development to be as distant from each other as
possible. The more explicit the top-down decree and the more

BEJING 798 MSC COURSE WITH SEUARCH NANJING
_Hyperbody 2006

distributed the bottom-up emergence behaviour, the stronger the tension field builds between the two forces. It is exactly this strong field of tension that I attempt to create in each and every design effort. The concept thrives in a strong tension field, the proposed object becomes an object of desire, even more so when that strange object of desire is positioned in an explicit environment where the object is the top-down body part and the environment is the distributed being.

The two opposing poles of the conceptual tension field are by definition acting on any building body design with bottom-up emergent increase of information, and top-down imposing of information on otherwise complex adaptive systems. Any system that reads data is, in reality, top-down informed, while any system that produces data behaves as a bottom-up device. Thus any input processing output (IPO) device possesses a balance between bottom-up and top-down processes. Typically, when a designer informs a design system to take a specific shape, that shape is not formed spontaneously. I realize that there are ways to simulate bottom-up self-configuration following the principles of cellular automata, but typically these automated design systems have top-down design constraints to behave in a certain way. The boundaries of their behaviour are defined preceding the running of the algorithms, and hence the outcome is limited to a predefined range of possibilities. A self-organizing design system cannot jump beyond its predefined system boundaries; it is by definition a voluntary prisoner in its own system. This also applies to executable cellular automata. Self-organizing design systems are often used to create variations on a theme, the theme being imprisoned in its system boundaries. If a designer wants to coin a different theme, the only way is to propose a different design logic, culminating in a new set of top-down definitions for that design system. Each new design concept is, in principle, a new top-down definition informing the rules of play of the design game. On the other hand there is no top-down design without a bottom-up systemic behaviour. Top-down and bottom-up are two sides of the same coin. The design concept sets out the boundaries, often in an intuitive and, as seen from the perspective of the system, in an arbitrary way. There is no reason to be critical of imposing top-down decisions; there is no reason to ignore the power of bottom-up forces. In the provocative design concepts both forces must be given equal attention and proportional nourishment, in a proper dynamic balance. Top-down decisions of designers represent the desire to stand out, the wish to be respected, to become special on their own terms, to compete for selection according to the principles of natural selection. The design may be the prettiest or the ugliest, the fittest or the weakest, the boldest or the most cowardly, the most original or the most boring, the loudest or the most modest, the most precise or the most vague, the tallest or the tiniest, as long as it is recognized it can compete for further evolutionary development.

016 EVOLUTION OF THE FRONT OF THE PEUGEOT 201 TO THE PEUGEOT 208

How fascinating it is to witness evolution at work. In my lifetime I have witnessed much of the development of the headlights of production cars. The Peugeot 201 was made in 1929, the 208 prototype is scheduled for 2012 after 80 years of evolution, taking nearly ten years per step in the evolution. I could have chosen other brands as well that would show a similar picture. The top four images belong to my parents' life, the bottom four to my own era. I drove a Peugeot myself, the 307 type, which I purchased because of its bold design statement for the headlights. The headlights were larger than life, at least as seen in the context of that time, around 2000. Now we are used to it, and feel the complete fusion of headlight and body is a natural phenomenon, yet it took almost a century of evolution to get there. In the 1930s, the body of the Peugeot 201 was still the old coach, with the fenders just added on to that coach. The headlights were a separate species derived from the gas lamps, mounted on bars between the fenders, and coexisted with the other individually expressed components. This was the time of the Bauhaus where each function was expressed as a separate element. In 1938 came the 202, and we saw an interesting feature appear. The headlights were still a separate species, but semi-hidden behind the spikes of the grille. Not many other brands chose this solution. The purpose was clear – to streamline the body to reduce drag. The fenders were cautiously merging with the hood, all components more rounded off. In the 203, the 1948 model, the merging process continued. The headlights were no longer a separate volume in space but pushed into the volume of the body, yet still round and clearly derived from the earlier lamp design. The logic obviously was that a lamp should be round, since the light bulb is round and it shines equally to all sides. Fenders and lower part of the hood were now made in one piece, the grille expanded into the fenders and around the lamps. By 1965, the 204 design had the headlights and the grille merged together as a combined unit pushed into the body, while the fenders were hardly expressed at all, as they were merged with the sides of the car body. But evolution did not stop here. It never stops, it keeps ab-

PEUGEOT
201, 202, 203, 204, 205, 206, 207, 208
_peugeot.fr

sorbing new technologies into the car bodies and it stimulates new desires in their designers. The designers learn from other brands and other consumer products, and apply their findings in the new prototypes. The 205 showed a new feature marking the beginning of a completely new exciting conceptual approach. The headlight now made the turn around the corner of the 1983 body. Finally the bumper had merged as well. Evolution at work is unbeatable, as the 206 design in 1998 set the tone for many other brands. The headlight became a fashionable eye, the grille a seductive open mouth eagerly inhaling the air so as to drive faster and faster. The notion of speed had definitively arrived in the generic production cars. The bumper was now completely merged with the car body.

Is this the end of an evolutionary lineage? Not at all. The concept of emotive styling comes emphatically into the picture in the first decade of this century, as was already clear to Chris Bangle when he designed the Gina prototype. And there are new technical developments for lighting technology, evolving towards LED lights that do not require much space. And of course the electric motor will be introduced soon, making the big mouth obsolete, and without a doubt leading to a new aesthetic. Now what about the evolution of building bodies?

HEAD TRUNK AND TAIL TRANSFERSTATION ELHORST / VLOEDBELT

_ONL [Oosterhuis_Lénárd] 1994

2.11 Generic and Specific

A proper understanding of the two negotiating forces is of prime importance for managing design steps that depart from the initial design concept. The internal design system represents the generic and agreed-upon values, while the concept represents the specific, the special, the uniqueness, the strangeness of the design. The specific informs the generic to specialize in a certain direction, while the generic in itself will not choose directions. The generic functions as a set of interacting cells that are subject to instructions, the generic is the swarm. The generic design

**ESZTERHÁZY
FERTÖD PALACE**
_ photo Martin Božik

system behind the Cockpit in the Acoustic Barrier is the principle
of triangulated doubly curved surfaces, described by the mathematics of nonstandard geometry as was defined in the 1960s by
mathematician Abraham Robinson. Yet the specific formal characteristics of the Cockpit design, the smooth elastic lines, come
from outside the system boundaries. The information to feed the
internal Cockpit design system comes partly from the environment, partly from the designer. They are the players that create
the parametric values to inform the nonstandard design system in
a complex game of interactions. Directly derived from and bilaterally connected to the double curved surfaces is the triangulated
structural system. The design system of the Cockpit is without
doubt generic. Yet the Cockpit is considered to be extremely
specific by our fellow practicing architects, since it deviates from
their commonly agreed-upon way of executing their otherwise
rectangular practice. But in fact the Cockpit is much more generic
than the majority of modernist designs systems, which are almost
by definition based on simple Platonic solids.
The infamous kidney shape as introduced by Le Corbusier seems
to be a wish to escape the severe limitations of the primary
solids. It eventually took the musician and mathematician Ian-
nis Xenakis to break Corbu's rules for the Platonic prison, when
Xenakis imagined the ruled surfaces of the Philips pavilion at the
Brussels World Fair in 1958. But the vast majority of architects
who regard themselves as modern remained voluntarily caged in
simple shapes. I could rightfully argue that they are still in denial
of the inclusive and generic nature of the evolution of nonstandard design systems and are unaware of its intrinsic generosity
towards lower-level systems. Nonstandard architecture is one
level up with respect to the modernist Euclidic world of geometry.
Platonic shapes can easily be described with nonstandard mathematics, but, let us face it: the other way around is dramatically
problematic and virtually impossible.

2.12 Similarity of the Body Plan

In carbon-based life forms the term 'convergent evolution' describes how life forms with a different ancestry may evolve similar traits, with different DNA structures leading to similar body plans. In the silicon-based product life in our daily environment of products and buildings we see convergent body plans as well. For example, car bodies follow an internal logic in their body plans in a way similar to buildings. ONL's garbage transfer station Elhorst/Vloedbelt (1994) features a head, a trunk and a tail part, very similar to a car with the front end containing the motor, the cockpit offering proportional space to the driver, and the tail part for carrying things and spitting out waste material. I was driving a Renault Twingo at that time and I was struck by the similarity. In car logic, motor and trunk part are typically narrower sectors than the driver's compartment. There are analogies that could be made to other input processing output (IPO) devices like computers and instruments. The front part takes in the information, the body part processes the information, while the tail part produces information in a different form, or carries information objects to other places as in the case of the trunk of the car transporting all sorts of objects from one place to another and thus informing the other places with new information. The driver of the car that is an IPO device is clearly the processor, interpreting the incoming data. Likewise the body part of the Elhorst/Vloedbelt garbage transfer station is clearly the processing part as well, since there the incoming garbage is sorted and reorganized. Hence the body plans of these very different species – car, computer, building – are to some extent similar, and can be considered to be a form of convergent evolution. There must be a generic logic behind the idea of a building body, similar to other bodies. And not completely surprising, similar to carbon-based bodies as well, as the similarity can be mapped all the way from single-celled to multicellular organisms and objects. The body plan of a feudal palace resembles that of an eagle in full flight, the main body and its connected wings spreading out to impress their subordinates. The grand entrance is like the beak of the greedy raptor bird, the spread wings represent the stables, inhabited by the horses and carriages to explore and exploit the country.

    The body plans as I have developed them in my practice are without exception vectorial bodies, bodies with a vector. Many consumer products can be understood to have a vector, from electric razors to airplanes, from coffee cups to cameras. To think of a body plan for a building body possessing a dominant vector is the logical consequence of considering the building body as a vehicle to go places, as a mobile space that is not an endpoint of your journey, but rather as a starting point for social experience.

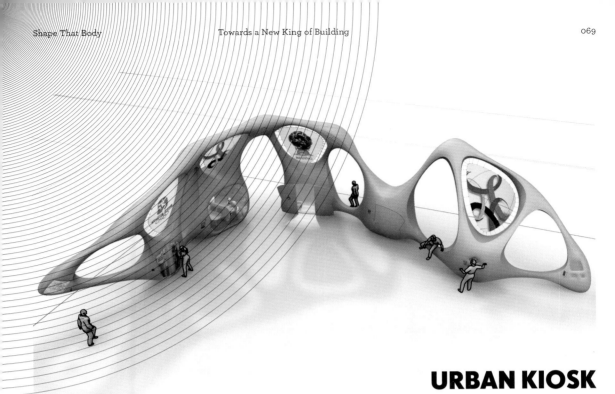

017 URBAN KIOSK GUANGZHOU

URBAN KIOSK GUANGZHOU
_ONL [Oosterhuis_Lénárd] 2007

We were invited to participate in the international competition for an urban kiosk in Guangzhou, China. The intention was to make 1,000 kiosks scattered around the city, in very different local conditions and in varying sizes. The concept is derived directly from the earlier art project called Windmask designed by Ilona for the Wilhelminapier in Rotterdam. The conceptual approach is to define a number of points in space, the point cloud of reference points, and map the nodal details with their varying functions on the points.

The design starts in an extremely unelaborated way by selecting a number of points in space. Then the parametrically prepared details of the nodals are mapped onto these points, making them all look like one big family. Then the individual points are assigned different functions, which makes some of them blow up in order to contain their functions, such as: toilet, vending machine, take-away bar, telephone booth, advertisement display. Then we wrote an elementary parametric script, informed by external data on functions and locations, to become a structure that could be seen not only as an independent sculpture but as a fully functional small building as well.

This fusion of art and architecture can be done at all building scales from small to large. A condition for its success is for the artist-architect team to have full control over the budget, meaning also having full responsibility for the artist-architect and their engineering consultants to make ends meet within the budget as given by the client. That responsibility is rarely granted, but is the preferred situation.

WEDDING CHAPEL NANJING

_ONL [Oosterhuis_Lénárd] 2007

018 WEDDING CHAPEL NANJING

Mr Lu, the CEO of Cipea development in Nanjing was personally very charmed by our proposal for a wedding chapel on a hilltop in the Cipea site, some kilometres outside of Nanjing and adjacent to a nature preserve area. But it has not been built, at least not yet, because a supervisor popped up in the person of Mr Isosaki from Japan, and he did not think that our project was feasible and so advised Mr Lu not to go ahead with it. Somehow he must have been misled by the extravagant costs of the neighbouring art museum designed by Stephen Holl, which we know was very expensive. Since our work looks much more complex, the general opinion of our work is that it will be even more expensive. But we know better as all our works have been built within the given budgets since we were able to utilize a Design and Build team that has full control over the generated geometry and the con-nected CNC manufacturing process, including the costs involved. We have always been able to evolve our designs without losing the elementary features, in a way that fits a given budget. The general problem is that decision makers all too often base their opinions on assumptions, not on facts. This is another reason to become more of an entrepreneur architect, with full control over the finances, the performance and the methods of produc-tion, rather than simply offering the design as a product. Artists already do that; product manufacturers work like that also. What holds us back as architects to find an investor, develop a product and sell it to the clients for an agreed-upon fixed price?

2.13 The Expert Formerly Known as the Architect

In Gehry´s architecture the structure is hidden between the exterior and the interior skin and is invisible as an architectural statement. In my view both the skin and the structure should be considered as active players in the repertoire of the designer, and hence that requires an active opinion from both the structural designer and the skin designer, which is most likely one of the key tasks of the expert formerly known as the architect. I have learned from the many student projects that I have initiated at Hyperbody that the new role of the architect is not easy to define. I have found that the new architect must, to start with, be an information architect. I support the vision of the founding father of liquid architecture, Marcos Novak, who described the new role of the architect as *sculpting data*. The organizational question in the multiplayer setting of collaborative design and engineering is if the architect will still be in the lead, as the architect used to be, as many retro thinkers are still hoping for? I support the view of direct democracy that all experts should have control over that sector of the building information model that fits the range of their own well-defined fields of expertise. In that model of cooperation all experts should be authorized to execute changes in the reference model within the limits of their own field of expertise, without the approval of any of the other experts. If anyone can propose changes from within their own well-defined disciplines, then how exactly must the discipline of the architect be defined? There are, of course, many tasks an architect can fulfil, but let us consider here the position of the *signature* architect, the designer who is leading in the definition and development of the first conceptual idea. For practical reasons I will consider the signature designer and his/her design team as one single identity. Imagine a swarm of experts involved in the early design process. The members of the swarm are exchanging their data via protoBIM or a similar immediate data exchange technology. Each member is authorized to impose changes on the protoBIM reference model, within the limitations of their own field of expertise.

So what should be the specific 'job description' of the artist formerly known as the architect? There are hundreds of specific tasks to be fulfilled, and one person, or one team of experts including the signature architect may adopt a number of these well-specified tasks. Analysing my own practice, I suggest that the following tasks be adopted by the signature architect. The new kind of architect launches the concept in several simple lines of script to be quantified in a few essential parametric values via the graphic interface of the script, which is directly linked to relevant external data feeding the quantitative aspects of the concept. During the fulfilment of the tasks the new kind of architect requires the active participation of other experts. This includes the financial expertise of the client to supply the designer with timely relevant data as early as possible in the design process. And includes the active participation of CNC-equipped manufacturers as well, for they are responsible for verifiable tender budgets based on precise data from the swarm of experts. Data must be verifiable, thus all experts will be held responsible not only for their qualitative and quantitative data, but for the financial logic of their expert input as well. Everything that is related to geometry must be the responsibility of the new kind of architect. And I indeed mean everything, including the geometry of the structure and the geometry of all components of the climate installation. When there is a debate on the shape, any shape, it must be the form-giving expert who is responsible. The engineering partners must calculate the quantity, performance and effectiveness of the flow inside the given shapes, be they spaces, structural components or air ducts. The geometry of things belongs to the realm of the spatial form designer, calculation to structural designer and climate designer. In actual building practice, some 20 to 30 per cent of the building budget is claimed by climate installations, the geometry of which is usually not at all controlled by the form designer but is developed away from the form designer.

Here is the most straightforward definition I can think of. Shape and concept is the domain of the former architect, performance and calculation is the domain of the former engineer. At the same time it must be underscored again that geometry and computation must be bilaterally connected from the beginning, in all possible aspects, to bring both the shaper and the calculator into the position of a creative designer. One can design with shapes, one can design with numbers, both are equally important. This straightforward definition of the work covers every possible act in the design process, and this definition certainly will allow for a better integration of the disciplines.

To call the designer a stylist has always had a negative ring to it, as if all the stylist would do was just a sort of decorative façade, In fact, when searching the Web for the word 'stylist', the first listings are for hairdressers. However, assuring that the stylist has an authoritative and decisive voice in everything that has geometry, including air ducts and arresting gravitational forces of the structure, would change the professional respect for the role of the stylist drastically. Everything that has a shape has a style; there exists no object without style. So the stylist must be allowed to become a respected expert. Just assume that the designer styles the building body, including the way the air flows and the way gravity is led through the structure, in a demanding way similar to how the car designer styles the car body. Yes, then we are talking, then the expert formerly known as the architect is back on track, forward to basics.

2.14 Synchronize Structure with Architecture

The fusion between architecture and structure leads naturally towards a radical new approach of ornamentation. In order to achieve that new approach, some radical conceptual design ideas must be implemented. For the design of the structure and for the architectural styling of the Cockpit we chose to synchronize the dimensions of the structure and the cladding com-

DRENTS MUSEUM ASSEN
_ONL [Oosterhuis_Lénárd] /
A&C / Technip 2007

ponents. It should be emphasized here that this is completely contradictory to common building practice, yet is still based on straightforward design logic and practical solutions. The longest tubular members forming the triangulated diagrid structure of the Cockpit are approximately 4.50 m, which is considered to be very small for a load-bearing structure of that size. In a typical column grid the columns are set 7.20 m apart, sometimes a little more as when, for example, the grid must accommodate parking spaces under the building, in which case an 8.10-m grid is typically chosen. In 99 per cent of the finished buildings in our world the façade system is added to the column grid as a secondary structural system with smaller dimensions representing a secondary order, to hold the vision glass panels and/or the non-vision parapet panels. Thus a separation of structure and façade system is created similar to the separation of functions in urban design, similar to the segregation of functions in modernist architecture, which is based on the logic of mass production methods.

In the Cockpit design, as in other nonstandard designs like the Web of North-Holland, the Acoustic Barrier, the CET and the Al Nasser Headquarters, my office embarked on another approach that has a number of clear advantages. The structural system and the façade system are fused into one. The dimensions of the glass and the spandrel panels are synchronized with the dimensions of the main load-bearing structure. This leads to larger dimensions than usual for the glass panels, and smaller dimensions than usual for the structural beams. The balance between steel and glass dimensions is thus found in the maximum possible dimensions of the glass and other cladding materials. The design principle is to shrink the diagrid system of the steel structure to fit the pumped-up glass dimensions. In combination with the approach of nonstandard customization that allows for wide parametric variety of the possible dimensions, the dimensions of the steel and the glass for the individual components are allowed to vary within a certain bandwidth of possible sizes. This process of dynamic synchronization between the main structural and façade systems is characteristic for designs of the nonstandard era, and especially characteristic of ONL designs. Ornamentation follows as a natural consequence of this approach. Ornamentation is synchronized with the main structure and the façade system, as they all stem from the same genetic origin, based on the concept of local specifications of the generic nodes.

2.15 New Building Species

In recent history, in which silicon-based objects represent the 'new nature', there are many examples of crossover manipulations, a form of fusion design. One species fuses with another, and that leads to a new species in the arena of product life. Take as an example the species of the sedan car and the small van, fuse them together and create the multipurpose vehicle (MPV – or, as it is known in the USA, the sport utility vehicle, SUV). This particular crossover fusion was brought to the market only 25 years ago by the introduction of the Renault Espace, and now all major brands have several types of MPVs positioned in all their market segments. This fusion must be regarded as a huge evolutionary success.

One of my own design strategies is to bluntly combine previously unrelated subjects or objects into something new, something surprising, into a new crossover species waiting to be checked and balanced by fast track evolution. The Cockpit as embedded in the Acoustic Barrier has lead to the definition of a new species of a stretched inhabitable acoustic structure. There have been precedents of the combination of building and acoustic wall, but they have been more like a hybrid structure, not properly fused into something new. While in a hybrid the constituent components can be clearly traced, in a true crossover fusion an entirely new image is born. Predictably, this new crossover species may eventually spread like a benign virus, since it will appeal to a range of social considerations in today´s society. The fusion stands for the multiple usage of the ground, it stands for sustainability, it stands for efficiency, it stands for innovation. It may take years, though, before the expert swarm of consultants and authorities have this type of crossover incorporated into their master plans, a necessary step before the new species can find fertile ground.

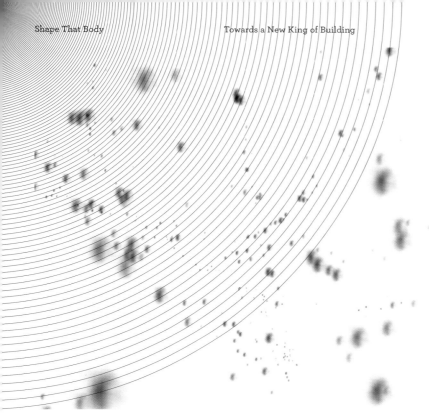

HANDDRAW-SPACE BIENNALE VENICE

_ONL [Oosterhuis_Lénárd] 2000

019 TRANS-PORTS HANDDRAWSPACE

Massimiliano Fuksas invited us to design an installation for the 15 x 15-m central room in the Italian Pavilion for the Architecture Biennale 2000 in Venice. In 1999 we stumbled upon a new type of software that intrigued us. We were already interested in software that would allow us to program a built structure that would behave like the Trans-Ports project we had simulated in a video for the Archilab Conference in 1999. One of our interns, Rich Porcher from France, showed us the Nemo software, a platform for game design, which was relatively easy to use since it works with a graphic interface that is easier for architects to grasp than plain straightforward scripting. We have worked with Nemo (later renamed Virtools, and later again renamed 3DVIA after being taken over by Dassault Systems) ever since at ONL and in Hyperbody.

For Venice, Ilona designed an Interactive Painting as one of the three modes that Trans-Ports could be switched to. She made an intuitive 3d sketch as a carrier of thousands of particles that were continuously sent out from the trajectory of the sketch. The public could interact with the sketch by walking around in the playing field between the three big projection screens, each of which offered a view of the three-dimensional, always changing world. Moving around meant the size of the dots was changed, which changed the numbers of particles, which changed the colour of the particle universe. Moving around was equivalent to changing a parametric value which was then processed by the NEMO software in real time.

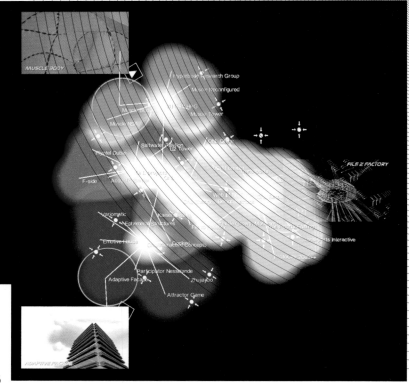

protoCITY 2005 ++ NANCY

_ONL [Oosterhuis_Lénárd] 2005 / Hyperbody

020 protoCITY 2005++

At end of the 1980s we proclaimed the fusion of art and architecture on a digital platform, and since then we have been invited to a number of events where we could elaborate on our vision. Jean Louis Maubant, the curator of the Nancy exhibition titled 'Avenir de Villes' invited artists-architects to participate. We designed a game to be projected on a circular playing field on which the public could play. By stepping on or near the marked signs on the soft field one could attract, rotate, repel and distribute coloured dots. Each dot had a sound sample (extracted from a piece by Liugi Nono) connected to it, thus choosing dots was constructing a music piece as well. The music would never repeat as there would always be a new combination of sound samples. Each dot represented an ONL project. Only when the dots were pushed to the perimeter would the corresponding image of the project be shown. The public, especially children, would figure out after a while how the system worked, and would play the game with the specific intention of bringing the dots to the perimeter so the projects could be seen. Playing the game was pleasant in itself, navigating through colours and sounds, but could also be used as a browser through the ONL portfolio. This project demonstrates the strategy of designing sculpture buildings, buildings that can be both an autonomous sculpture and a properly functioning building as well, such as Sculpture City 1994. In protoCITY 2005++ interactivity is mapped on matter in much the same way. The interactive installation is recognized to be an autonomous piece of art as well as a perfectly functional browser.

2.16 Fusion of Art and Architecture

Beginning in the late 1980s and together with Ilona Lénárd, I embarked on an uncompromising fusion of art and architecture, all of it on a digital platform. Since then we have developed a radical theory and practiced that theory in numerous projects, many of which have been built. We started mapping dazzle paintings to housing schemes, fully covering their façades. We developed the radical paradigm that in the fusing of art and architecture both disciplines should obey two primary rules. The first rule was to place art and design on the same scale, since we no longer accepted art to be a small precious brooch on the bosom of an otherwise much larger building body. The work of art should cover at least the entire surface enveloping the spatial structure. The second rule was even more obtrusive into the traditional categories of art and architecture. We stated that both disciplines should work with the same budget. No longer would art be a mere 1 per cent art in the front of a 100 per cent architecture building. From then on it was to be 100 per cent art fused with 100 per cent architecture. This bold and challenging statement eventually culminated in the Sculpture City event in 1994, after earlier design hypotheses for a complete fusion of her art and my architecture. After the Dazzle Paintings for the Patio Housing at the Dedemsvaartweg, The Hague (1990), De Kassen in Kattenbroek, Amersfoort (1991) and the Dancing Façade in the Hunze, Groningen (1992) the implementation of the new paradigm of sculpture buildings followed soon after to its full extent in our practice. The Saltwater Pavilion at Neeltje Jans and the Web of North-Holland were built in 1997 and 2002, respectively. Thus a new kind of practice was born.
In the first decade of this century the notion of sculpture buildings has become widely accepted and acclaimed among other architects, and was soon to be popularized by the Gehrys and the Hadids, and vulgarized by mediocre architects. Unmistakably the virus was spread, the evolutionary battle was won. As a popular by-product of the art of sculpture buildings the word 'iconic' architecture was introduced during this decade.

One of the basic conditions of being an artist is that one has full command over the budget. When art is commissioned the artist gets a pot of money and then is fully responsible for producing a work of art with a value corresponding to that amount of money. The contract between the client and the artist is based on trust. When the artist and the architect team up in one consortium, each of the two is responsible for only that part of the job that is subject to their exclusive authorization, although the threads of each of their authorized actions are in a complex way intertwined with the other expert's threads. This organizational model where disciplines have become delicately interwoven is reflected in the very complexity of advanced design proposals. It is a natural by-product of the constructive attitude of the players in the serious design game that they have no problem being an active member of a larger design team. The members work together in a contractual framework that must, of necessity, be based on trust – trust that the other experts are performing to the best of their knowledge and abilities. New contractual frameworks must be devel-

MPV RENAULT ESPACE_
_wikipedia.com

oped to facilitate the new roles of the new kind of designers. This
is evolution at work. In the building industry recent developments
favour an even more responsible position for the selected party:
DBFMO (Design, Build, Finance, Maintain and Operate) consortia
are given full responsibility for the whole enterprise for a period
of 25 to 30 years. The leading party in DBFMO contracts is usually
financially the strongest party, usually the bigger contractor. I see
it as the task of the new kind of nonstandard architects to claim a
position in such consortia to include financial responsibility for
everything related to style, shape and geometry, and, above all,
the concept. In such larger consortia we must operate on the basis
of trust, fully responsible and capable to deal with it financially,
which is in turn based on specialized expertise. When you are a
true expert, you know what you are doing, why you are doing it,
how to do it, and what it costs. The artist knows, the new kind of
architect knows.

2.17 Iconic

The notion of sculpture buildings is now more alive than ever,
despite recent destructive efforts by retro-activist Rem Koolhaas
to discredit signature design schemes, a weak attempt of his to
force the spirit of today back into the bottle. Time will prove his
misjudgement. Art and architecture have definitively been successfully fused; new species have emerged to stay. In his sour
attempt to justify his own uneasiness in dealing with nonstandard
complexity, Koolhaas has declared iconic designs to be a disgrace
for architecture. But in this statement Koolhaas has used a false
definition of the term 'iconic'. The term iconic itself has nothing to
do with buildings featuring complex geometry. A perfect cube can
be iconic as well, a cube with a round hole can be iconic, an OMA
structure can be iconic. Koolhaas uses the populist technique of
making overly simplistic pronouncements, such as linking the
word iconic to curved feature lines, when these two terms obviously have no relation to each other. To declare the existence of
such a relationship may seem similar to the earlier described
combinatory fusion techniques, but this is really different. There
is no value added by combining the iconic with the curved, on the
contrary, it loses meaning. It makes our language dumber. I do not
see any enrichment in this kind of hybrid. It warps the designers
back in time, a retroactive act indeed. Wasn't that the subtitle of
Koolhaas's first book *Delirious New York, A Retro-Active Mani-
festo for Manhattan?* I remember how much I disapproved of his
stance back when he gave his first lecture at Delft University of
Technology, and how much I regretted (a feeling that has become
stronger and stronger with time) that he has since lured a herd of
young designers into the dead-end modernist retroactive track.
Not only has Koolhaas given a false notion of the iconic, he also
shows no understanding of the limited number of iconic structures actually built in the world, and in the Emirates specifically. I
estimate that for every 1,000 buildings built in the Emirates there
may be one building that could rightfully be described as iconic
in the narrowest sense of Koollhaas's interpretation of the word.
Only one! Is that worth raising a voice against the iconic, or does

**SPACE XPERIENCE
CENTER CURACAO**
_ONL [Oosterhuis_Lénárd] 2009

that justify his own aversion to the new complexity, the one based on the principles of mass customization?

Any attentive designer these days naturally takes advantage of the new potential of industrial customization. A designer who stands in the vibrant life of 2010 does not look back in nostalgia to the era of mass production. There is no need for it, and it certainly it does not move our society in a forward direction, not even to basics. Indeed, Rem Koolhaas has attempted to trivialize the word iconic, and has again successfully driven a large number of architects into the dead-end street of populist banality. Koolhaas may be remembered as a modernist conservative and a nostalgic post-modernist manipulator in the history of built architecture, albeit an influential one with an army of admirers and followers who are impressed by his commanding presence in the architectural arena. It is not completely accidental that in the 1970s he advised his young students to read the hedonistic novel *The Fountainhead* by Ayn Rand (1943), a notoriously conservative writer and philosopher of capitalist objectivism.

2.18 protoSTYLE

The concept designer must have an opinion on style. When Googling the word 'styling' the first ten images address hair styling, followed by interior styling. When Googling 'body styling', car styling emerges as the winner, in the sense of tuning, or adding accessories to the body, but nothing on the essential styling of building bodies. I introduce it here as something important and I will advocate for a deep emotive styling of the building body. Styling always needs a body to work on, be it a body of hair, or a body of a car. The term styling is usually used to indicate an after effect, adding style to an existing body of hair, or an existing car body design. Therefore I feel the need to specify the meaning of styling further and introduce the term protoSTYLE, meaning applying style-related gestures while the body is being shaped, before it is made, using personal style elements while modelling that building body in 3d.

In these paragraphs I will make my case for a professional approach towards the protoSTYLEing of the building body. I admit that protoSTYLE themes usurp most of my time as the lead designer of ONL's building bodies. The exact trajectories of the feature lines have always been my prime interest, since they organize the point cloud of reference points, the basic material the designs are made of. My attention is often directed to the dynamics of the smooth appearing and disappearing of the feature lines, to the expressive nature of the fold lines, to the powerlines shaping the boundaries of my personal design universe, to the inlays, to gently embedded coexisting species of building components, to the force transfers from one building component to the other, to the continuity of the powerlines and the fold lines, to the transitions from convex to concave surfaces, from smooth to angular, from flat to double curved. My attention focuses on establishing bold cantilevers, on establishing a unification of materials and details. One building, one detail, that is the message. Also this is a choice for considering style in the first place, as it is undisputedly a factor in innovative design and building techniques as well. In the following pages I will explore the vast number of protoSTYLE opinions as applied in the ONL designs, which were typically activated from the very beginning of the design concept.

2.19 Feature Lines

A car designer usually starts by sketching powerful feature lines to characterize the body traits, to evoke robustness or elegance, to advance the notion of muscles or speed. The curves of the feature lines map emotion on the car body. Let's look closer at some curves recently featured on the sides and fronts of car bodies. In the evolution from the Peugeot 201 to the 208 series, the sides and fronts of the car have become connected to form one continuous whole. No longer are car bodies developed with a separate front, side, top and back design. Indeed, modern feature lines continue all the way around the body, connecting the back lights to the sides to the fenders to the headlights to the bumpers, often in one stroke. By comparing the different individual treatments of the curves one can see what intention the designer had in mind when sketching the curves in 3d. Analysing the styling of the new Citroen C5 and comparing it to by the Chris Bangle-controlled BMW styling teaches us how the feature line activates the volume of the body, and how different styling attitudes have a different effect on the emotive character of the body.

The 3d feature curve of the side of the C5 is full of tension. It feels like a strained 3d arch, evoking the restrained power of a leopard before it leaps, curved as seen from above and as seen from the side. The BMW curve is a straight line from the side evoking a more aggressive wedge shape, cutting the air at fast speed. The C5 communicates a different message than the BMW; the strained arch evokes the *promise* of speed, building up tension before the big leap, while the BMW curve evokes the feeling of being *in* speed, slicing the surrounding air. The Volvo S60, no longer in production, displays another interesting approach towards the 3d curve moulding the car body. This line is not prominently visible as a line but is more of a soft moulding force pushing the overall shape of the side into a rounded curved arch. This volumetric bend connects the two wheels with a bow-shaped softly rounded ridge, thus internalizing a sort of distributed four-wheel traction capacity to evoke robustness even when there is not a four-wheel drive in reality. The message is that of canned power, a message of civilized strength. Indeed, car designers are trained to have an opinion on the curve and their emotive expressive effects. So it is also up to the information architects to have an opinion on their curves, but not before acknowledging that the building body designers need a body in the first place to map their design efforts upon. Oscar Niemeyer has already showed us a way; he applied his personal opinion on the curve on *in situ* moulded concrete structures. Now information architects need to develop their personal visions on curves as applied to mass customized tailormade building bodies and their constituent building components made of steel and glass, composites, or virtually any other material that can be CNC produced.

**SHEIK ZAYED
ROAD
DUBAI**
skyscrapercity.com /
photo Imre Solt

2.20 *My Personal Curve*

Niemeyer's curves are born from nature, crystallizations of the contours of the mountains of Rio de Janeiro, reflections of the contours of female bodies on Copacabana Beach. Niemeyer draws his curves as an abstraction from observed natural curves, and then stretches them to describe the full length of his buildings. In his otherwise linear functional language his curves, almost by definition, end with straight line segments, while the central part is usually curved in a regular fashion, as a fillet between two straight end segments positioned at an angle to each other. The contours of the conference halls of the National Congress in Brasilia end in a straight line, the two parallel curved bars of the University of Brasilia end in two straight legs at either side. That is his signature curve, his feature line, the curve as designed by Niemeyer. No one has tried to copy his simple and powerful curvature since no one has emotionally *felt* the curve like he did.

If curves are that personal, I must ask myself what is the nature of *my* personal curve? While indeed I have an opinion on the curve, I have for a long time sympathized with the manner in which Niemeyer ends his curves. But in the mid-1990s I chose to empower the two opposing poles of my building bodies more explicitly. I did not want my curves to end like loose strings as Niemeyer does. My curves feel like they are held strongly and slightly pulled by a strong force at either end of the curves, straightening the curve a bit but not completely, just enough to evoke muscular tension. In geometrical terms it is more like ending into the tangent to the straight line than in ending with a perfectly straight and lengthy line segment. Also the middle part of the ONL curves are not simple 3d fillets, they are more freely curved in 3d space. The 3d trajectory behaves in a more complex way. Seen from different angles it behaves differently. The curves form trajectories in space, not as a set of parallel curves, but rather as smoothly diverging and converging curves along a 3d trajectory so as to pump up the volume they are describing, and to be bundled together again at the two poles. My curves are not controlled by my preconceived imagination. I cannot imagine the curve exactly inside my brain without tracing it in 3d space; it cannot be drawn on a flat piece of paper. I need to have it modelled in 3d to develop an opinion about it. Since Niemeyer had no access to computation he had no other choice than to control the curve inside his head and execute it with the movement of his hand on a piece of paper, while I can take advantage of the computing power of the PC and indulge myself in the enormously increased potential of all possible curves by weightlessly navigating in 3d space, tweaking the control points of the curves. The thousand-fold increase of all potentially powerful curves does not make the job of the protoSTYLER easier, but certainly more interesting and more challenging. I must dive into the quantized space/time of multiple possibilities. I must find my direction intuitively, and during the spatial exploration develop my personal opinion of the curve to finally act as a professional and experienced building body protoSTYLER. I know that realizing a building body defined by such curved powerful power lines is possible since I also know that it can be directly transcribed into reality using digitally driven manufacturing methods. If I had not been familiar with these new customizable CNC production techniques I would not have even dared to develop a personal view on 3d curves.

2.21 From Kandinsky to Bezier

Kandinsky had an opinion on the curve. In his prophetic book *Point and Line to Plane* written in 1929, he proposed a scientific approach towards the basic components – point, line and plane – of the profession of painting. He considered the *point* to be the proto-element of painting, and talked about the self-contained repose of the point. He considered the *line* to be the greatest antithesis of the pictorial proto-element, the point. He stated that the line represents the leap out of the static into the dynamic. Line is movement. To Kandinsky even straight lines represented movement. He saw the curved lines as straight lines drifted out of their course by constant pressure from the sides, by negative (downward) or positive (upward) pressure. He thus considered curved lines as deformations of straight lines. But I have a different position. Instead, I see straight lines as poorly informed curves. I look at the line from one level up, and then look one level down, which is a commanding position. From that point of view the straight line is the most unlikely configuration of all possible curves. I conceive of the straight line as an endless parametric rope where all the thousands of parameters defining the thousands of points on the curvature are constrained to one and the same value, thus straightening the curves into a line.

　　In mathematics the straight line is defined as the shortest distance between two points, which is a Flatland version of the line. In the Spaceland version the straight line is the minimally informed reduction from the potentially heavily curved appearance of that line. Likewise the flat plane is seen as the reduction of any topological double-curved surface. The sphere is of all possible volumes the most unlikely and has the maximal reductionist configuration. I see the sphere as a poorly informed volume where thousands of parameters are set to one and the same value. The perfect sphere is the exception to the rule, the singular state of a dynamic swarm of connected points in space. There is a progressive mathematical description for curved lines. Kandinsky was aware of that too. Nowadays one works with the notion of the spline, the bspline and the Bezier curve, all unknown in Kandinsky's time. To describe, for example, the Bezier curve one needs to imagine vertices and handles placed outside a visible trajectory, like attractors or repellers having influence on the course of the line. First Paul de Casteljau, at Citroen in 1959, and Pierre Bezier at Renault in 1962 used the splines for the design of car bodies and Bezier has published on the parametric nature of these curvatures. Bezier needed the new definition of the curve to enhance his design-driven control over the smoothness of curves and double-curved surfaces. In car body design the curves are often delicately stretched to almost, but not entirely straight lines. The control of the curve which is just *slightly* bent has been the important driving force in developing the Bezier curve. The control over *slightly* bent curves to me is top priority, since it introduces a level of precision and subtlety into the design process that was until then unknown. That precision is what we focused on when designing the A2 Acoustic Barrier with the embedded Cockpit showroom. Since the cars are passing by at a speed of 120 km/hour, the driver experiences the curvature in a telescopic view that gradually unfolds in an upbeat tempo along the stretch of the motorway, as compared with the designer's view from sitting behind the computer monitor. The designer needs to adopt new techniques supporting a sort of augmented sensitivity for the nature of long stretched elastic lines and needs to internalize the speed to feel the curve.

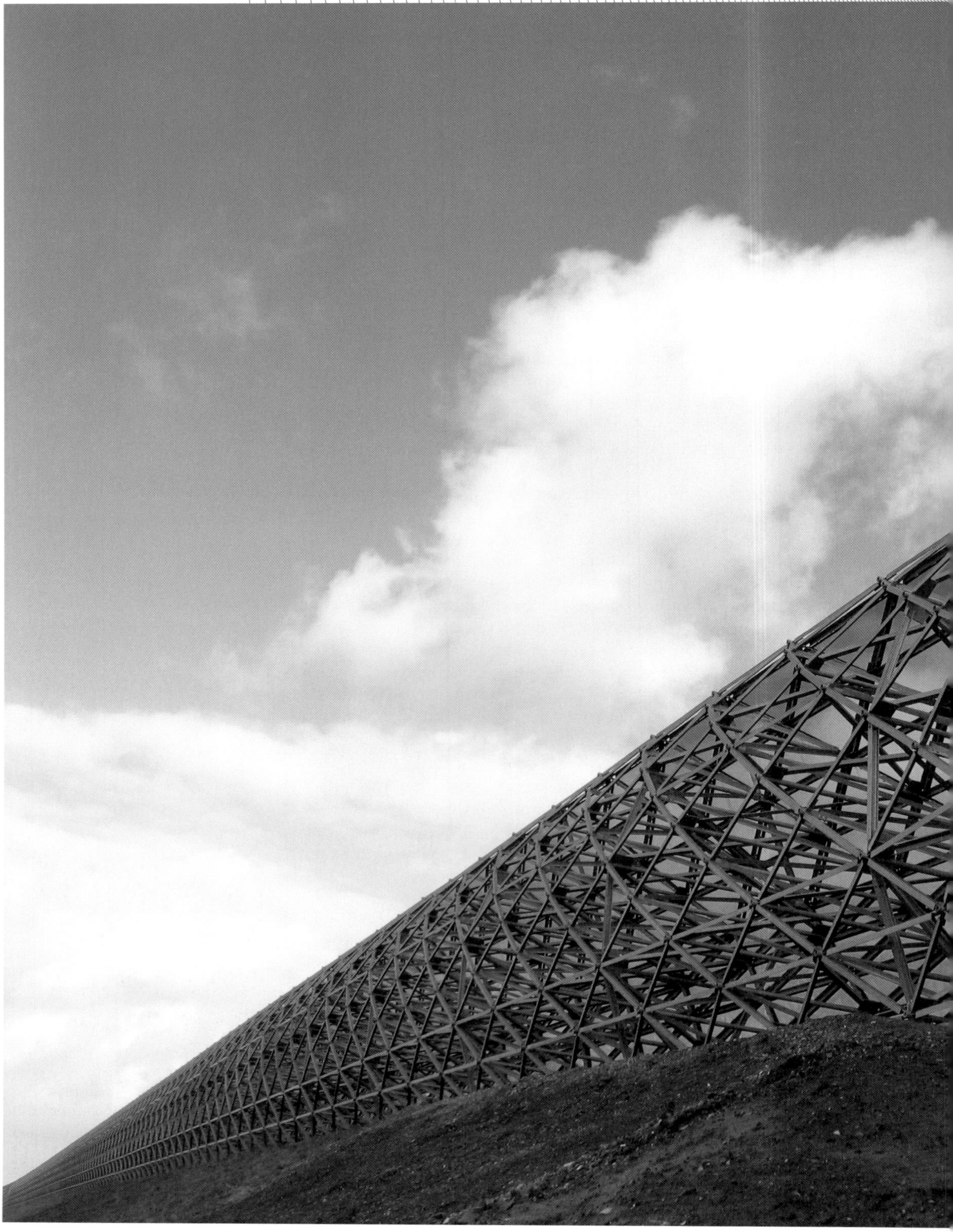

ACOUSTIC BARRIER ALONG A2 HIGHWAY
_ONL [Oosterhuis_Lénárd]
2005 / photo Kas Oosterhuis

52° 06' 46'' N
5° 02' 39'' E

POWERLINE BUILDING #1 WAITINGI PARK WELLINGTON
_ONL [Oosterhuis_Lénárd] 2005

021 WELLINGTON POWER LINE

We developed the strategy of powerlines directly from the fast and intuitive sketching method of Ilona Lénárd. The powerline obviously is the line that has the force. The line has been informed by a powerful gesture; it generates power when applied to the mouldable mass of a building body. Since the gesture follows a curved trajectory in space, the powerline is curved as well. Once the powerline is sketched using the 3d digitize, it becomes clear how it works. The 3d digitizer software places a selected number (parametric value) of points while tracing the line in space. Making the gesture then equals placing a series of points in space, which are subsequently used to define a spline curve running along the points.

In our design for the invited international competition for the buildings in the Waitingi Park development in Wellington we decided that the powerline would function as the spine of the buildings. The volume of the restaurant plus climbing wall compound was tweaked along the curved spine. The powerline/spine served as the reference line for all further design decisions; it formed the so-called mother curve. When changing the trajectory of the mother curve (law curve) the total volume changed with it, since it follows the spline of the spine. For the Wellington designs we chose to position the spine at the outside of the volumes, thus enabling us to control the outlines of the buildings during the design process. We applied the same technique for the two other buildings of the Waitingi Park development, thus creating a strong family of building bodies.

022 CET POWERLINES

CET stands for Central European Time, and 'cet' is also the Hungarian word for a whale, so this is what the public nicknamed our design – the glass whale. There has been a lot of wordplay in the press already, mostly in a positive way, since the shape and the name refer to something that is huge, but soft and friendly. The design for the CET commercial and cultural centre in Budapest is based on a number of powerlines, demarcating both the contours of the building body and the fold lines. The top line shapes the contour of the project from one side to the other. The powerline runs from the top of the entrance up in-between the two existing and renovated warehouses to the back of the body and then makes a turn all the way to the ground, along its downward movement pointing back so as to create the imposing cantilever. At the sides there are two powerlines, one more dominant than the other, but both following the same logic. The upper fold line is the extension of the top of the pitched roof of the old buildings, while the lower fold lines are the extension of the gutter of the old buildings. The CET body plan is fully symmetrical, like car bodies, like vertebrate bodies, like bodies of consumer products. Powerlines serve a similar function as the often curved feature lines in the emotive design of modern cars. The curvatures we chose for the powerlines always end in a straight tangent, they always fade out into endlessness. That is our personal opinion on the curve that we apply consistently as a deliberate strategy in our designs.

CET
BUDAPEST
_ONL [Oosterhuis_Lénárd] 2007

NATIONAL CONGRESS BRASILIA
_Oscar Niemeyer /
photo Kas Oosterhuis

2.22 Personal Style

Any prolific designer develops a personal proprietary style. Signature architects develop specific styling elements that they may rightfully call their own, although they would also be, in an evolutionary sense, derived from the styling strategies of other or earlier designers. Designers must develop their own personal styling language to stand out, to excel, to become recognized as a signature protoSTYLE designer. For the new, almost virgin, field of nonstandard architecture it is far from obvious what the styling features exactly are of the self-proclaimed nonstandard designers. I can only speak for myself, and compare that which I am interested in to what others seem to be doing.

The young designer Domagoj Dukec, who sketched the new C5 sedan, introduced a specific styling element that is omnipresent in many details from dashboard to door handle, from headlights to back lights. The shape of that styling element is something resembling a stylized pistol, a hand with a pointed finger, a bird's wing, somewhat boomerang-shaped, consisting of a substantial body with a slightly tapered and slimmer pointer, all with their edges rounded off. These references may be far-fetched, maybe inaccurate, and they may not be what the designer himself was thinking. Yet they clearly refer to the desire for a streamlined body with built-in motion and aggression, definitely a desire for a shape with a dynamic vector.

I cannot avoid reflecting on my own personal styling elements, and among many examples the styling of the U2 Tower comes to mind. The curvature defining the tension of the back spine of the U2 tower is a complex curve, with inflections and deflections, combined with a hyperactive rotating behaviour at the armpit. The powerline along the top of the glazed roof of the conference centre bends actively downward to the point where the horizontal conference sector prepares to become a vertical tower, makes a sharp but rounded U-turn, and bends upward and slightly forward to describe the back spine of the tower, all the way up to the forward jutting tip of the U2 recording studio.

2.23 Not the B-Word Please 2001

To avoid any misunderstanding I must, with much reluctance, discuss the obnoxious B-word, and only once here in this book. An alien shapeless thing called the Blob that transported itself through the smallest keyholes and swallowed everything was introduced by the movie *The Blob* (1958). The alien here represented the ultimate threat to bourgeois life. The Blob could only be brought down by exposing it to extreme cold, by freezing it. And not completely coincidentally, this is exactly what Greg Lynn promotes when describing his animated but, in effect, motionless blobs in his book *Folds, Bodies & Blobs*. Lynn uses animation software to generate blobby shapes and then he literally freezes the motion. The conclusion must be that Lynn finds pleasure in killing the aliens, like a hard-boiled Texas cowboy in a B-movie. But I like Marcos Novak's attitude towards the alien so much better. He welcomes the alien; he deliberately creates the alien so as to surprise himself and his audience. This confronts me with something new and unexpected, and stimulates me to improve myself. Think of the apes getting smarter after having been confronted with the super-smooth rectangular alien shape in Stanley Kubrick's *2001: A Space Odyssey*, 1968.

Superficially observed from the outside and not bothered by facts, one could possibly assume that ONL's work is similar to Lynn's blobby shaped animated bodies, but in fact I feel much more sympathy for Novak's aliens. ONL does not imagine or fabricate blobs at all, and there are good reasons why that is not the case. There is the other true meaning of a blob, which is the blob as a Binary Large OBject, in computer architecture lingo indicating a bag full of data, without knowing exactly what is in the bag. ONL knows exactly what is in the bag, and therefore is not designing blobs in this sense either. Then there is the popular meaning of the word blob – a rounded off, somewhat randomly-shaped volume, a three-dimensional inkblot, a Barbapapa creature, a streamlined potato, like Jacob MacFarlane's restaurant in Centre Pompidou. This is *not* what ONL and Hyperbody make; their volumes are treated as unique industrial products with precise attention to the styling of the body. Not a single viewpoint escapes a thorough scrutiny; the body is observed and validated from all sides and from many different angles. The styling of the body is based on a deeply felt opinion about the curve, both the sharper fold lines and the smoother roundings. True nonstandard building bodies are not a random result by a beginner modelling for the first time in 3d Studio Max or Rhino, as initially beginners tend to be fascinated by the fact that the software works at all. Nonstandard experts are far beyond that stage. Blobs are for dummies, nonstandard architecture is for protoSTYLE professionals. Please do not use the B-word when I am in your immediate neighbourhood as I may find it offensive and develop a bad temper.

RENAULT CARAVELLE

_renaultcaravelle.com

BIRDS
ON A WIRE
_photo Rie Itou

023 BIRDS ON POWERLINES

The first meaning of a power line is, of course, the electric cable that distributes thousands of volts from power plants to factories and households. But we use the word powerline to indicate the power of the curved feature line, a 'high voltage' line intended to influence the shape of things to come. When the swarm birds land in an organized manner on the powerline, it still is a swarm of birds. They still behave like actors following simple rules in the swarm, like Craig Reynolds' computerized boids. They still share the same direction (very few land in the opposite direction), they still respect an agreed-upon distance from their neighbour, they still try to sit close to the middle of their swarm. But there are some parameters set to zero, there is information missing. There is no longer any speed, they sit still. As a consequence there is no longer a real time adjustment to the changing positions of neighbours. The intriguing part is that it is still the same swarm, following the same rules, but it is now top-down informed by the powerline. This is exactly the power we have given our powerlines, our feature lines that organize the points of the point cloud of the reference points being used or created for the definition of our building bodies. The powerline is introduced to the point cloud system as a force from outer space, forcing its power on the swarm of points, forcing them to organize themselves along the powerline, at agreed distances, to describe a smooth but powerful bspline, with the intention of it functioning as the spine of the body.

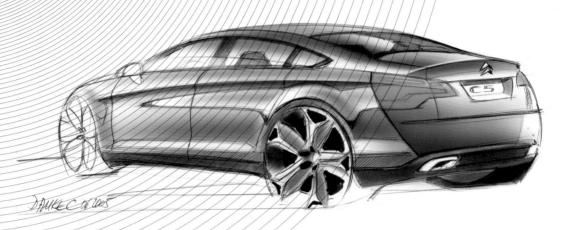

024 FEATURE LINES CITROEN C5

Electrical power lines are passive; they hang from electricity masts. But the powerlines for our buildings, and the feature lines of car bodies are active lines; they contain the power of the strained arch, of the leopard bowing its back before it leaps. The C5 feature lines evoke power and the promise of speed. They communicate the promise that the power will be unleashed and transmitted into speed, such as when the cat hits its prey. As in all artist impressions of car bodies the dimensions are distorted, the wheels are oversized, the body more voluptuous, the windows smaller than in reality, so as to leave it no doubt what the design intention is. The feature curve on the side originates from the front wheel to emphasize that the front wheel drive train transmits the power to the asphalt. On its way to the back of the car the curve avoids the rear wheels and connects directly to the taillights, while the deep fold caused by the feature line is transferred into the taillights themselves. From there a complex set of relations between the car body components is established. The taillights (and the headlights) have that specific shape characteristic of many components in the C5 styling – not a single shape but an hybrid form, with a body and a pointer, like a pointed finger and the hand, like a pistol, so as to evoke a sense of direction in the individual component. The taillights go around the corner and have a firm grip on the back part, unifying all components into a larger whole. The unique hollow-shaped rear window is included in the unifying styling of the tail.

2.24 *Framing the New Kind of Building*

In politics *framing* is known as the technique to promote a message in strong one-liners that tolerate no objection. Objecting to the explicitly framed message brings the opponent into a defensive situation, one that is typically judged by the public to be a weak position. The purpose of framing is to overwhelm the opponent, to communicate that resistance is futile. The now suddenly popular and at the same time frightening Islam-bashing is a typical example of political framing. The framing technique stems directly from the advertisement business. In politics, the spin doctors apply this technique to promote the political ideas of their candidates. It would be naive to think that in the profession of architecture the message can be delivered in a totally neutral, objective, non-emotional way. Projecting this observation back on myself means that I need to frame novel ideas about nonstandard architecture in a professional way in order to profile myself. At present, the technique of framing is used against the concepts of industrial customization and nonstandard tailor-made architecture. The words *blob* and *nonstandard* also work slightly against us since they inherently possess a negative connotation. The B-word refers to the uncanny ravaging aliens, to destruction and the fear of the unknown. By contrast, I think of something positive when I think of our double-curved designs, when I think of the beneficial potential of ICT-driven architecture applying complex geometry. But the power of framing is huge. When I defend myself and declare that I am not making blobs, then I am using the B-word. So I must avoid using the B-word at all. For me, the introduction of the *Blob* lab at Delft University of Technology (borrowing the word *Blob* from the title of Lynn's book) hurts. It is painful and counterproductive for an unstrained understanding of ONL's work. Besides the framing force of that annoying word, there are architects such as Massimiliano Fuksas and Erick van Egeraat who make rather opportunistic drawings of complex shapes, without taking into consideration the necessary link from file-to-factory, without linking their designs to the knowledge required about CNC production methods, and hence impeding the acceptance of nonstandard architecture by the larger public.

If my designs and buildings are not blobs, how then should I refer to our designs? It is not just the B-word that works counterproductively when discussing the new kind of building. It is the very word *nonstandard* itself. Nonstandard analysis is a branch of mathematics that formulates analysis applying infinitesimal numbers, based on integral and differential calculus. The popular meaning, however, is that nonstandard is different from standard or customary and is *out of the box*. The problem is that the word 'nonstandard' describes something which is *not,* instead of what is. Therefore, for the sake of sending a positive message subject to the rules of framing, I feel obliged to find a better word for 'nonstandard'. Let us give it a try. In Dutch we might consider the word *maatwerk*, which means custom-made in English, or tailor-made. But custom-made does not make reference to CNC production methods, as it should because of the intrinsic relation between nonstandard geometry and CNC manufacturing. 'Complex' is not an option either since that sounds too much like something that is complicated, although it is not. In my view complicatedness is exactly the opposite of complexity, which is, by definition, based on simple rules. Although I repeatedly illustrate the obvious difference between complexity and complicatedness in my lectures worldwide, the word 'complex' still does not sound sufficiently positive when used separately from its counterpart 'complicated'. If not a blob, if not nonstandard, if not complex, then what? Maybe we should go for 'augmented' architecture, analogous to augmented reality, which clearly refers to information and communication technologies (ICT) in daily reality, so augmented architecture could mean being informed and with value added by our digital culture.

Or maybe I should chose from one of the earlier titles of lectures I gave worldwide during the last decade, such as *The Exception Is the Rule, Mies Is Too Much, Speed And Friction, The Idiot Savant, Swarm Architecture, Building Relations, If You Are Not In Real Time You Are Dead, Out of Control, Immediate Architecture, Mass Customization, From Point Cloud to Real Time Behaviour, Protospacing Architecture, Powerlines, Quantum Architecture, Architecture Is Construction Is Ornamentation, Cold Fusion, Body Building, Instrumental Bodies, Artificial Intuition, Working Space, Body Styling, Hyperbodies, The Synthetic Dimension, Vectorial Bodies, The Road Map from Nonstandard to Interactive Architecture, ONLogic, What Exactly Is Nonstandard Architecture?* Such titles would all be relevant and adequate. And they all refer somehow to the existence of a New Kind of Building. This forward-looking title has a positive ring to it, although it does not describe exactly what it is. The label *New Kind of Building* promises the new, yet doesn't reveal any of its content; that is up to the reader to find out.

2.25 *Emotive Styling*

Do not blame the Chinese for copying when you yourself may be the biggest thief of others' styles. A decade after we initiated our Trans-Ports projects, after having presented my inaugural speech at Delft University of Technology in 2001 titled *Towards an Emotive Architecture*, after we designed and built a number of interactive prototypes at Hyperbody using pneumatic pistons provided by Festo, I saw the BMW Gina prototype designed by Chris Bangle on the Internet. He first presented this prototype in 2009, although in fact it had been designed back in 2001. While Gina itself was a well-kept secret, in the years of Chris Bangle's design leadership over the BMW styling centre Gina functioned as the inspiration for his design approach. With Gina, Bangle introduced a new character for the feature lines, evoking a linear force from within the car body that pushed the skin of the body outward, much crisper than was previously known in BMW styling. He gave BMW a younger and more aggressive character, full of energy and emotion. I will come back to Gina in the next section on programmable architecture where I will elaborate on the adaptive and proactive behaviour of building bodies. But apart from the electronic pistons inside the Gina that are, in real time, adjusting the curves as to evoke emotional values, the frozen instances of

THE BLOB 1958

_wikipedia.org

the living Gina were in itself perfectly capable of enhancing the emotional potential that Chris Bangle wanted the BMW car bodies to supply.

Car design in this decade has become the celebration of customized emotion, which, as a concept, comes before defining customized manufacturing. Some years before Bangle invented the Gina, in 1999 I presented the Trans-Ports programmable building body at the first Archilab Conference in Orléans. I presented Trans-Ports as a multimodal building capable of changing shape and content in real time. Since I published it just before the Millennium shift, Bangle may have been familiar with the idea, but I am more inclined to think that this is a nice example of convergent evolution. During the interview by ONL senior architect Gijs Joosen with Chris Bangle for the third issue of Hyperbody's *iA bookzine* series, Bangle said that he believes architects are more forward-thinking than car designers, which I found remarkable since I tend to think the opposite. But he may be right after all, since indeed *avant-garde* architects can instantly absorb new developments and quickly apply them in built prototypes. They are relatively free to realize their ideas, assuming they can find a client to support their radical concepts. Cars are basically still mass-produced products in large series and are hence subject to more severe market constraints and to longer incubation periods. However, we are now seeing a turn to smaller series and less time-consuming production in cars as well, a process that will be stimulated even more by the introduction of electric cars and the desire for higher emotional values for the car. The green computer numerical control (CNC) revolution has entered the world of cars, and may speed up the paradigm shift towards full customization for virtually all consumer products.

TRANS-PORTS V1 ARCHILAB
_ONL [Oosterhuis_Lénárd] 1999

2.25 Forget about Pilotis

In the late 1980s it was obvious to me that architecture needed a new approach and I began thinking of the building as a building *body*. I have illustrated that new approach in writing about the need to implement actual ICT technology in the art of building, and showed in an essay in *OASE* in 1991 that all five points of the modern architecture of Le Corbusier have become obsolete. The Villa Savoye stands for values that are no longer viable. Le Corbusier relentlessly promoted his five points: *pilotis*, free plan, horizontal windows, free layout of the façade, and roof garden. Looking at my own building bodies, I see that they are never built on *pilotis*, that they are structurally self-supporting, and that there are no columns. Both my flat floor buildings and my buildings with undulating floors (the Saltwater Pavilion) are without exception column-free to allow for maximum flexibility in the interior. Columns would spoil the play of forces that are taken care of by the structural shell. This design approach applies to BRN Catering (1987, in collaboration with Peter Gerssen), Elhorst/Vloedbelt (1994), Saltwater Pavilion (1997), iWEB (2002), Cockpit (2005), CET (2010) and Al Nasser HQ (2011). Rotterdam-based architect Peter Gerssen taught me to avoid internal columns, and I have been very consistent in this approach since day one in my own practice (almost scary when looking back.) Thus no columns, no *pilotis* in ONL's buildings. While the free plan concept may still apply to our flat-floor designs, certainly horizontal windows and free layout of the façade have become irrelevant old-school recipes. One can easily recognize modernist architects since they still by and large stick to Le Corbusier's hang-ups. The information architect should, however, strive for a full fusion of architecture, structure and ornamentation, which allows for a much greater spatial freedom and a much richer architectural expression than the free façade, a concept doomed to live on as a miraculously surviving crocodile in an obsolete flatland. The free façade concept has degenerated in modernist architecture into purely decorative random additives to an otherwise rigid column-and-beam structure. Roof gardens are not relevant either, since they assume a flat roof in the first place. Flat roofs are incompatible with the very concept of building bodies, which naturally feature curved roofs in order to move along with the variable inflation of the interior volume. Naturally this argument also applies to pitched roofs.

Instead of the five Corbu points I could substitute this: *A building body is a self-supporting system composed of unique components, spatially defined by complex geometry, informed by external and internal parameters*. This design philosophy is worlds apart from Le Corbusier, who is at the other end of the design spectrum, as far away as possible from all modernist pastiches that are basically, in their flawed nature, poor copies of Le Corbusier. Forget about *pilotis*, do not accept interior columns. Teach yourself not to look through the distorted lenses of the still omnipresent post- and after-modernist practicing colleagues, whose minds seem to have lost contact with the changing world around us and hence are doomed to drift away in twentieth-century or even nineteenth-century nostalgia.

WEB OF NORTH-HOLLAND ART MODE FLORIADE
_ONL [Oosterhuis_Lénárd] 2002 / photo Kas Oosterhuis

025 WEB OF NORTH-HOLLAND SPACESHIP

Spaceship, monocoque structure, no columns, minimal footprint, big cantilevers, fold lines, building body, CNC fabrication, one building one detail, architecture is structure is ornamentation, nonstandard geometry, complexity following simple rules, the exception is the rule, file-to-factory, dry assembly of bolted building components, industrial customization, all components unique in shape and dimensions, there is only an entrance when you need one, a new kind of practice, collaborative design and engineering, design and build, product design, feature lines, parametric design, informed point cloud, personal universe of reference points, scripting, inclusiveness, multiplicity, opinion on the curve, crossover fusion, sculpturebuilding, buildingsculpture, both art and architecture, not a blob, a new kind of building, vectorial body, powerlines, radical concept, cellular structure, protoBIM, quantumBIM, second life, demountability, collaborative design and engineering, participation, interactivity, sensorium, hyperbody, real time behaviour, swarm architecture, instrumental body, cold fusion, the exception is the rule, Mies is too much – all this is applicable to the design, engineering, fabrication, and assembly of the Web of North-Holland, commissioned in 2000 by the Province of North-Holland and curated by Tituts Yocarini of the Cultural Council of North-Holland. It opened its giant doors in 2002 at the Floriade World Expo, was then purchased by Delft University of Technology for a symbolic one euro, and resurrected in 2008 to function as the protoSPACE 2.0 laboratory of Hyperbody.

026 WEB OF NORTH-HOLLAND ART AND ARCHITECTURE

WEB OF NORTH-HOLLAND ARCHITEC-TURE MODE FLORIADE
_ONL [Oosterhuis_Lénárd] 2002 / photo Kas Oosterhuis

There is only a building when you need one. When not a building it is a sculpture. The Web of North-Holland is only a functioning building when the giant doors are open to form the canopy. When the doors are closed there is no indication that it is a functional building. There are no visible glazed windows, the door does not look like a door from any catalogue, there is no indication at all that this is a building. So it must be something else. The spaceship only reveals its function as a building when it is actually functioning as a building. When the building is closed it does not function as a building, which allows it to serve another purpose.

When Leen van Duin, then Head of the Department of Architecture of the Faculty of Architecture of Delft University of Technology, told me at the opening of an exhibition of our work that to him the Web of North-Holland is art, I felt offended and found his opinion disrespect-ful. Naturally I took the position that the Web is serious architecture, that it is an icon of nonstandard architecture, that it is a new kind of building. But now I know it is both, it is both art and architecture at the same time. This is typical of a sculpturebuilding that can turn into a buildingsculpture. Doors open, it is architecture; doors closed, it is art. One simple canopy door marks the switch. Thus we learned that built structures can change modes by turning a switch on or off. The Web of North-Holland marked the important first step towards buildings that can change their modes of operation by electronically switching them into other modes, like zapping through TV channels.

2.27 Yes We Build Spaceships

Imagining a building body as a load-bearing monocoque frame instead of a building on *pilotis* with a rigid internal grid of columns opens up a completely new field of dreams, techniques, styling exercises, skills and contextual dialogues. When buildings are no longer seen as rising up from the ground, but rather as making a soft landing after arriving from weightless space, most of the old design techniques will no longer be valid. No more *firmitas*, in the classic meaning of the word. While being strong and robust, my building bodies are conceived as self-supporting structures, produced as an industrially customized product. Yes, we build spaceships, spaceships that are conceived in weightless digital space, calculated as if a vertical force was drained through the structure to simulate gravity in preparation of its projected landing on earth. During the process of conception the spaceship body has been in virtual contact with the site, establishing a dialogue by exchanging relevant data like coordinates, volume, weight, expected arrival time, local ground conditions, local climate conditions, accessibility of the site, all administered by the parametric protoBIM software. The landscape where the spaceship intends to land will be prepared to provide for a soft landing, embedding the structure seamlessly into the existing city fabric.

Since all building components of currently built structures come from far away, not a single building is built of local materials extracted from the local site anymore. Those were the glorious days of the Dogon people. Why not accept that fact and acknowledge the reality that a building is a universal spaceship, building up a special relationship with a local site, trying to the best of its knowledge to communicate with the local language, while still speaking the alien language from the universe from whence it originates. New buildings are by definition the 'other', the immigrant, they are the allo-body. Accepting this wholeheartedly as a fact changes the attitude of the designer and leads towards positively embracing the notion that buildings are friendly spaceships by their very nature. Accepting this fact stimulates the designer to nourish the building body concept as long as possible in weightless space while looking for a proper architectural expression for the building body, and then to send it off to interact and negotiate with the local environment.

2.28 Vectorial Bodies

No longer does one step into a building body as designed by ONL the same way one enters traditional buildings. Traditional buildings are entered through the front door, as in temples and castles, or as in housing typologies derived from temples and castles. In ONL's building bodies you step in sideways, as in car bodies, as in airplanes, as in trains, as on your bicycle. In monocoque building bodies you enter sideways and then you go places. The building body is the vehicle to beam you up to other worlds. Building bodies are uncanny yet canned imaginary worlds. To be able to take you places, the building body is a

SALTWATER
PAVILION
NEELTJE JANS
_ONL [Oosterhuis_Lénárd] 1997 /
photo Kas Oosterhuis

vectorial body, a body with an intention, stretched in a particular
direction, heading for that other unknown world.

In general one could argue that the sequence of entering a
building, experiencing a stay inside that building, and stepping
out again will transform one into another person. In between
entering and disembarking the experience is processed, the visitors themselves are processed, and carry new information to the
outside world. Buildings, cars, airplanes and bicycles are typically input-processing output vehicles. Normally I use such sequen-
tial process description exclusively for intelligent programmable
buildings, but in essence this is true of static structures as well.
Projecting the knowledge of today onto the world of yesterday,
I cannot deny that static buildings are also information processors. The main vector gives a direction to that process. Thus the
experience of a stay in a static building as compared to a stay
in a vectorial building is not the same. A person who enters a
square or round building and stays there for a while experiences
something different than a person in a vectorial building body.
Vectorial bodies will appeal to your desire to go places, you will
feel more stimulated to act and explore. The vectorial body as a
whole entity may affect you to become active, but it is also perfectly possible to imagine a number of spaces inside a multicel-

lular building body that are designed to come to a complete rest. Thus a dynamic balance can be created between the desire to explore and the need for relaxation. The day before yesterday the consumer economy was dominant, yesterday it was the experience economy, and today the transformation economy is on the rise, asking people to use emotive environments to transform themselves. This is the key to the client of today, the modern client pays the designer to transform their business. Dynamic vectorial buildings are the appropriate vehicles to drive the participatory transformation economy.

2.29 On-Off

A feature of the iWEB of which I am personally fond is the double meaning of the building body. The iWEB is both an autonomous sculpture and a well functioning building – robustness, usability and beauty in one. When the door annexe canopy is closed, the viewer sees and appreciates the iWEB as a sculpture, a piece of art. But when the door annexe canopy is *open*, the viewer is invited to step in, and appreciates the structure as a functional building, an architectural piece. The iWEB is alternately sculpture and building. Door closed: sculpture. Door open: architecture. The most intriguing part of this on-off design strategy is yet to come. When one analyses traditional static canopies, the building makes an inviting gesture, as if to say 'Come in please'. But if that door is locked, then the invitation is made just the same but entry is denied. In psychology this would be considered to be conflicting information. At the same time that the building with the fixed canopy communicates that you are welcome to enter, the door remains closed, and there is no way to get in unless you have the key. But only a few privileged people have that particular key, thus effectively excluding you and many others as members of the unwelcome majority. In the case of the iWEB, the fusion of art and architecture makes it possible to send out this wonderful elevating message, that the structure only exists as an accessible building when the canopy is up. When the canopy is down the structure does not exist as an accessible building anymore; then it is the iWEB as a sculpture. You would not even attempt to get into a sculpture. There is only an entrance when you need one, when you need the iWEB to be a building.

2.30 Minimize the Footprint

Is there a reason why so many ONL designs feature a spectacular cantilever? Yes, and that design strategy took off as early as 1988, while planning cantilevered box-like volumes for the XYZ towers for the centre of Paris within the *Périférique*. The three axes, one vertical (Z) and two in the horizontal plane (X, Y) materialized into an asymmetric 3d cross of rectangular bars. The idea was to have a minimal footprint, thus illustrating the strategy of urban acupuncture, *acupuncture urbaine*. The structure was indeed feasible and checked by our structural engineer DHV, but in the course of our journey in the international architectural arena Ilona Lénárd and I decided not to proceed with this rectangular, somewhat modernist architectural language. Instead Lénárd and I embarked from

**WORKSHOP
CATALUNYA
CIRCUIT CITY
BARCELONA**
_ONL [Oosterhuis_Lénárd] 2004 /
Hyperbody / ESARQ

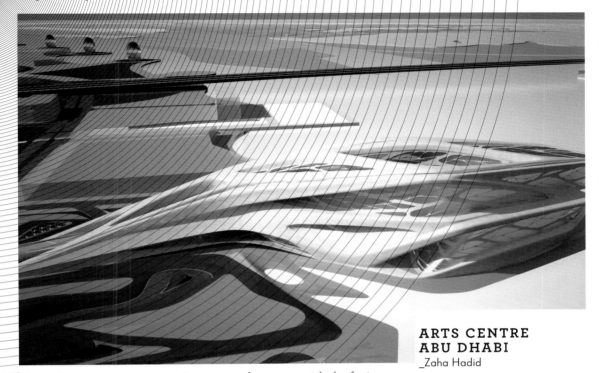

**ARTS CENTRE
ABU DHABI**
_Zaha Hadid

the early 1990s on an innovative new road, starting with the fusion of art and architecture, followed by incorporating the language of nonstandard geometry and later making a conscious decision to design robust and sustainable building bodies, including a strong sculptural expression with substantial cantilevering of parts of the body. The cantilever can be explained by the design methodology itself. The BIMs of ONL are, as an agreed-upon rule, conceived in weightless space, free floating in the parallel world of the digitally augmented space of the imagination. In weightless space one designs spaceships, since gravity is not yet an active force. What happens when the spaceship approaches its destination site can be described as a dialogue between the 3d model and the site by exchanging relevant data in such detail that the building body will land with high precision. How does this process affect the shape and the footprint of the building? Minimizing the footprint is accomplished by jutting out substantial parts of the heart of the building body. Since the building is not growing up *from* the site, but rather lands *on* the site, there is no reason to cover the whole site with its footprint. On the contrary it is much more likely that the friendly alien prefers a reduced footprint, so as to touch the ground lightly, minimizing friction. Minimizing the footprint imparts a definite *green* quality. It reduces the foundations drastically. Foundations are typically the least sustainable parts of any building since the reinforced concrete is usually firmly anchored to the ground, the piles are difficult to remove, the cast *in situ* concrete almost impossible to recycle. The iWEB has a projected area of 250 m², but the footprint is no more than 150 m². That is a reduction of 40 per cent, meaning a 40 per cent improved performance in this aspect of sustainability. Minimizing the footprint pays off.

iWEB
protoSPACE
4.0 LAB
_ONL [Oosterhuis_Lénárd] 2008
/ photo Kas Oosterhuis

**51° 59' 49'' N
4° 22' 35'' E**

**WEB OF NORTH-HOLLAND
'THERE IS ONLY A CANOPY WHEN YOU NEED ONE'**
_ONL [Oosterhuis_Lénárd] 2002

2.31 Second Life

There are many more inherently sustainable qualities to be found in ONL's work, but I have never advertised this since I think of it as a natural by-product of what I am really intrigued by. The clean, fully controlled file-to-factory Design and Build process guarantees reducing waste to the minimum, while the dry assembly of its unique tagged components means a fast construction time, saving substantially on interest losses. All waste materials such as steel, glass, and polystyrene are recycled directly from the workshop. Dry assembly of prefabricated unique components also facilitates a possible second life on another site. Obeying the rules for demountable buildings, the vectorial body of the spaceship building is ready to move on and find another site that is prepared to be its host for a period of time. This is exactly what happened to the Web of North-Holland. After its first life as a pavilion on the Floriade World Expo in 2002, it was purchased by Delft University of Technology for the symbolic amount of one euro, disassembled into the constituent tailor-made components and after a few years re-erected to become the iWEB and to be the home of the protoSPACE Laboratory of my Hyperbody Research Group at the Faculty of Architecture. The iWEB's second life unfortunately did not last longer than a few months. Although the iWEB itself was left untouched, the dramatic fire on 13 May 2008 caused the rescue team to pull the plug on the iWEB. Since then it abides at the edge of a desolated piece of wasteland on the destroyed property, hoping to be granted a third life.

2.32 Force Fields

Contrary to what is usually assumed by architecture critics, ONL designs have a strong relation to the context. Granted, the signature designs are not contextual in the traditional sense, as they do not follow boundary lines set by urban designers. What matters are the force fields that have shaped the place, what counts is to accept these force fields as a source of information influencing the development of the weightless juvenile BIMs. Retroactive analysis of a typical ONL design shows how force fields affect their building bodies. At first glance the Saltwater Pavilion might look like a stranded whale, one might even think that this had been the leading metaphor in the design process. But nothing is less true, the design did not start with a metaphor, the design task was not approached from superficial exterior features. The colour of the Saltwater Pavilion indeed is black and its shape somewhat reminds one of a whale, and the location is close to the sea where the whales live. But in no way did I think of a whale when I started designing back in December 1993. My first sketches were made during a visit to my family in Budapest, and there was nothing like a whale in that sketch. I mapped a diagram of gradual transformation from freshwater to seawater on the site, including both the NOX and the ONL part. I chose to design the sea sector of the water cycle. What I really did was empathize with the force fields of the site. I wanted to feel the forces that had shaped the site. I wanted a building that originated from the sea, that gave the impression it had been conceived in floating sea space before it got to Neeltje Jans. But *not* a whale, instead at that particular time a sea-born ship rather than a spaceship. Naturally a streamlined shape is fit for that concept. I applied the new language of liquid architecture to the building body in *statu nascendi*. Characteristics of the sea were included in the very genetic material of the Saltwater Pavilion in a multitude of ways: large building components were shipped to the building site across the sea, the interactive interior is supplied with streaming data from a weather station on a buoy at the sea, the black shape rests directly on the rocky shores of the sea and is embedded in the dunes. The feature curves culminate in a small horizontally stretched window pane that allows visitors to have a panoramic view of the inner sea, the fold lines fade in and out as in streamlined bodies, the volume of the body is pumped up in the middle, the trunk allows for a spacious indoors, with the Wetlab representing the below sea level world and the Sensorium the world above the surface of the sea. Thus the context is embedded in the genetics of the BIM, the genes being defined by the immediate external environmental factors. The other forces defining the DNA sequence of the Saltwater Pavilion arise from the interactive experience involving the visitors inside. Hence the architectural body is defined by an enveloping semi-permeable membrane positioned between the force fields of the internal and the external factors. There is a delicate balance between forces from within and forces from without, both sculpting data of the information model of the building. The design strategies of nonstandard geometry, of transformative fluidity and my preference for the alien are translated into the global universal forces working upon the foetal BIM.

2.33 *Polarization, Voltage, Massage*

As I have discussed earlier, there is a balance between the polar sets creating powerful force fields, between top-down and bottom-up, between sculpture and functionality, between static and dynamic. It always has been my aim to stretch the balanced forces to the extremes of their bandwidth, to increase the tension in order to feel the emotional voltage in the realized spaces. It must be emphasized here that I do not regard these balancing forces as opposing quantities, but as values at the two extreme ends of the same continuous scale. The not-so-hidden agenda of the ONL design strategy is to stretch the balancing values as much as pos-

SPANISH PAVILION SHANGHAI WORLD EXPO

_expo2010.cn /
photo Kas Oosterhuis

027 SPANISH PAVILION SHANGHAI WORLD EXPO

I still regret that my father did not take me to the Brussels World Fair in 1958. I wonder what effect that would have had on me as a 7-year-old. My father was a truly modern architect (modern, not modernist), making his best works in the late 1950s and early 1960s. My mother was an artist who painted dreamy flowers. Why didn´t they take me there? It could have changed my life. I had to discover the Atomium later, and recently I received one of the original aluminium skin panels of the Atomium as a gift from Sylvie Bruyninckx of Conix Architects, who handled the renovation. Last spring during a business trip to China we went to see the Shanghai World Expo. The Spanish pavilion designed by Bernadetta Tagliabue is one of my favourites. Thousands of hand-woven wickets are applied as big scales on the gridded steel structure. The pavilion is nicknamed 'The Basket'. I am sure it won't stand there for a long time since the material for the exterior dress simply will not hold. The design flirts with the nonstandard paradigm, but is really not nonstandard at all since the geometry is not generated from a populated surface but from a simple projection on the curved surface. The overall shape seems to be subject to a dynamic wave configuring the mouldable structure. The design flirts with contextual force fields, although it does not use environmental data at all. It will not be remembered as an icon for the new paradigm shifts towards the nonstandard and the interactive, yet it is a great building, because it radiates a carefree but powerful impulse to 'just do it'.

028 BRITISH PAVILION SHANGHAI WORLD EXPO

The British pavilion will be the one I will remember as the icon of the Shanghai Expo. From a distance the design intrigued; up close it intrigued even more. When walking up and down the sad Happy Street, Holland Pavilion designed by John Körmeling, it is virtually impossible to keep one´s eyes off the British Pavilion. Once inside via the fast lane, the center piece of the British Pavilion, called the Seed Cathedral designed by Thomas Heatherwick, proves to be a masterpiece. Then we were invited to take the fast lane. Indeed the design concept of the hairy soft cube is revolutionary. The experience both from the inside and as seen from the outside is multidimensional. Many layers of meaning can be seen in this splendid fusion of art and architecture. The Seed Cathedral, as it is called, is an object formed from 60,000-plus transparent acrylic rods containing unique seeds. The seeds demonstrate the concept of sustainability, the diversity of nature and the potential of life. During the daytime, each of these 7.5m long rods acts like a fibre optic filament, drawing on daylight to illuminate the interior. At night, light sources embedded in each rod allow the whole structure to glow. After the Expo the rods will be donated to as many primary schools in China as there are rods, thus involving almost the complete nation in the project. A concept could hardly stretch the imagination more than the tension field between the ultra-high-density implosive containment of the seeds and their future explosive extensive distribution.

BRITISH PAVILION SHANGHAI WORLD EXPO

_expo2010.cn /
photo Kas Oosterhuis

sible to the extremes in order to create polarization and voltage. The concept of the Saltwater Pavilion is basically defined by its two polar sides, between which the warped space is pumped up and stretched to enhance the tension even more, very much like a magnetic field is caused by the two opposing electromagnetic poles. The induced voltage intends to draw the public's attention to the special character of the environment, to make the public more alert to the spatial *massage* of the Saltwater Pavilion. The word massage refers of course to the true title of Marshal McLuhan's famous book *The Medium is the Massage*. (Please note that the original title of the book is *not The Medium is the Message*, which is probably the most misquoted slogan ever. Even when one sees the true original title, one is still tempted to read the erroneous version.) *The Medium is the Massage* fits my design strategies very well, especially with respect to the interactive light and sound experience inside the Saltwater Pavilion. It is truly a massage for the eyes and the ears.

MEDIA MASSAGE SALTWATER PAVILION
_ONL [Oosterhuis_Lénárd] 1997

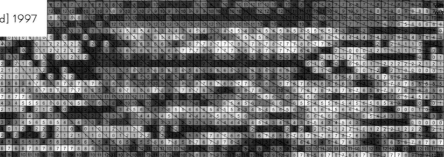

2.34 *The Building as a Product*

When we dive deeper into the aesthetics of a typical ONL design, we find a number of design strategies active at a more local scale as well. Some of these design strategies have been described in greater detail in my earlier essay 'Vectorial Bodies' (Archis 6/1999). I will repeat the keywords of the illustrative cases here for the sake of a comfortable redundancy: *Jaguar S-type: Input-Output, Ford Ka: Babylook, Chrysler Pronto Cruizer: Feedback, Hyundai Euro-1: Continuity, Ford Focus: Active Lines, Audi: Cold Fusion, Peugeot 206: Transmission of Energy, Fiat Multipla: Interface, Mercedes A: Real Time Behaviour, Smart: Unibody, Renault Mégane Family: Formula, Citroen C3: Pump up the Volume, Nissan KYXX: Streamline, Renault Vel Statis: Folded Volume, Citroen Xsara Picasso: Inlay, Chrysler 300M: Evolution, Lanci Dialogos: Consciousness.*

The keywords represent explicit design opinions that are acting on the BIM at the scale of the building body itself, like the earlier described design strategies dealing with curvature, nonstandard geometry, minimizing the footprint, polarizing, customizing, file-to-factory manufacturing, inclusiveness, multiplicity, e-motive values, crossover fusion, art and architecture, design and engineering, design and fabrication, structure and ornamentation, rules of the game, and naturally the radicalization of all of the above. I am particularly charmed by applied design techniques that prominently show (although not exclusively) in car styling. Many of the discussed design techniques can be found in product design at large. It is not surprising that I am in favour of a participatory design and manufacturing process producing buildings as a product rather than as a consultancy. Studying products gives me a pleasant feel for how design strategies to develop buildings as products may come to life.

2.35 *Learning from Car Styling*

Forces are imposed on the transformable digital matter of the foetal BIMs – forces that come from the inside, similar to the drive to grow up, and forces that are imposed on them from the outside. Also there are forces that travel from one part of the building body to another part along the enveloping surface, forces that transfer a gesture. In car design the sketching of feature lines from one end to the other and around the corners is a routine modelling routine. Fold lines in the fenders are continued in the head lights, while fender and lights serve a completely different function and are made of completely different materials. Yet the force that causes the fold travels from the one component to the other. The desire for continuation and unification is stronger than the individual expression of individual functions.

How different this is from traditional modern architecture, where the functional components are explicitly expressed as such. Staircases and elevator shafts are separated from the housing/office slabs. There is a dominant preference for the classical base/shaft/capital divisions instead of choosing one unified whole. Canopies and balconies as separately expressed components are favoured at the expense of components that are integrated in the overall shape of the body. Traditional modernist architecture could not be more different from the exciting practice of car styling. One could theorize that the aesthetics of modernist architecture is based on the aesthetics of car body designs from the 1930s. At that time all the functional components were expressed as such. The main body, the fenders, the hood, the head lights, the spare wheel, all components were clearly separately developed, and then simply put together. Car body design has long since overcome that simplistic design approach, and has even speeded up since the early 1950s. It is about time for the practice of architecture to leave that early mass-production aesthetic behind as soon as possible, and to start exploring the potential of specialization through industrial customization. Therefore I identify so completely with the art of car body styling, since I also adhere to design strategies that enhance the unity, the integration, the fusion, the continuation, the streamline, the emotive styling of the body. Once having chosen monocoque structures in my architectural designs, I have thereby systematically chosen to apply styling elements from product design practices, and car body designers in particular. Force transfer is an inherent symptom of product body design, the logic of the unified whole dominates the logic of the individual expression of constituent components. From this point of view all design operations that favour design ideas such as simple stacking of boxy volumes, rotating of boxes, cutting chunks out of a volume, punching holes, adding boxy elements to façades, randomizing windows, imitating Bart van der Leck's patterns on a façade, arranging a series of different sized boxes together, randomly scattering boxy volumes on a brown field, are all so OMA, so hopelessly old school, or so evidently decon, so blatantly in denial of the reality of today's design and manufactur-ing potential.

3.

> *Move That Body*

building components are actors in a complex adaptive system

3.1 From Mass Production to
Industrial Customization

My Nonstandard Architecture (NSA) practice, ONL, has been building
a new aesthetic based on the principles of industrial customization.
The principle of customization needs explaining as it is crucial for
further understanding of the concept of interacting populations. Mass
customization is the natural approach as seen from the perspective of
CNC production methods. The logic of customization linked to CNC
production requires that all building components possess unique
identities, that they are individuals that can be addressed individually.
In a building based on the principles of NSA not a single building
component is the same as another. Each one is different, each component fits only in one place. First the building information model (BIM)
and then the actual built structure are giant 3d puzzles where each
piece fits exactly in one unique location. The unique number of the
component is comparable to the unique IP (Internet Protocol) address
of a computer linked to the Internet. Architecture based on customization acknowledges the individuality of each component and builds a
completely new aesthetic. The most obvious effect of NSA is that we
no longer celebrate the beauty of repetition or a series of the same.
One must realize that all modernist architecture, from Le Corbusier to

**SENSORIUM
SALTWATER
PAVILION**
_ONL [Oosterhuis_Lénárd] 1997

Herzog de Meuron, is based on the outdated production methods of
mass production. Although many critics think differently, deconstructivists like Morphosis and Gehry also have developed an aesthetic
that still leans heavily on mass production. What they do, essentially,
is start from a series of mass-produced components and then impose
many exceptions, in other words they cause complicatedness. They
cut out holes, they slice off, they chamfer and twist, they superimpose,
they collide in collage, they build in conflicts, all as attempts to indi-
vidualize the components. But creating uniqueness in this brutal old-
school fashion is such a tragic mistake, such a waste of energy. What
irritates me is that the deconstructivists violate their materials and
production methods instead of working with them. The more logical
approach, consistent with the principles of customization, is to instead
synthesize architecture based on scripting and generative procedures,
and to take advantage of the file-to-factory (F2F) processes and CNC
production. Then each different shape is no longer an exception but
one of many possible instances of the rule. The design rules are for-

mulas mapped onto structures, surfaces and volumes, by definition open to changing parametric values. For the computer running the scripts and the computers plotting out the F2F half-products, each individual component is treated according to the same procedure. CNC machines do not care which numbers and parameters change from one component to the next. CNC machines adjust automatically. This is the first paradigm shift.

SMART PARA-METRIC TILES protoDECK

_Hyperbody 2010

029 protoDECK

protoSPACE 3.0 opened its doors in May 2010, as part of Delft University of Technology's BK City. While protoSPACE 2.0 was basically an augmented projection space in the iWEB, like the Trans-Ports installation at the Architecture Biennale 2000 and the Sensorium of the Saltwater Pavilion, protoSPACE 3.0 has the protoDECK, a smart floor that supports transactions with the surrounding augmented projection space. protoDECK is the joint effort of two of Hyperbody's high-potential researchers, Mark David Hosale from California and Marco Verde from Italy. Hosale designed, installed and programmed the hundreds of pressure-sensitive brains that are built into the floor. Verde designed and CNC manufactured the raised floor, which features a force-field pattern of customized floor tiles. Thus protoDECK has become a unique piece of nonstandard and interactive architecture in itself, containing the seeds for a range of applications. protoDECK serves as a prototype for a new generation of raised floor systems, a floor with embedded intelligent agents, with hundreds of small brains connected to each other like the birds in a swarm. The mini-brains read, process and transmit data to their nearest neighbours, while the collective signals are wired to an external brain, programmed in MAX MSP software. protoDECK also serves as a prototype for a new generation of customized floor tiles, subject to force fields that shape the unique components. All components possess a unique identity, both in the manufacturing process and in their real time behaviour as active members of the swarm.

030 protoSPACE 3.0

*The protoDECK floor with its embedded brain grid inside the
protoSPACE 3.0 laboratory facilitates, among other things, the interactivity between public and speakers, the interactivity between
the different stakeholders in a design process, and the interactivity
between dancers on the dance floor. protoSPACE 3.0 is used for
education, research, art projects and as a web lounge for mental
diversion. The smart floor shows how domotics may take shape in
our future homes and offices. No longer do we need to think of a repetitive pattern for wooden or composite floor tiles, since they can
be customized to take any shape, as long as their dimensions are
within the bandwidth of possible dimensions of the addressed CNC
production machines. The same industrial customization potential
applies to walls, ceilings and furniture-sized objects inside the new
domestic and commercial landscape. They can all link to the same
datascapes to share relevant data for their production. Customization may possibly lead to an extreme diversification in interior
design, similar but better then that realized in seventeenth- and
eighteenth-century palaces. 'Specials' are no longer a privilege of
the rich; industrial customization brings visual richness to billions
of twenty-first-century consumers. Think of embedding intelligence
in unique components in such a way that your immediate living
environment becomes an exobrain to augment your daily life. The
spaces themselves will become aware of their users and their individual profiles, and can adapt accordingly. Your immediate living
environment will become a third skin, equipped with many senses.
protoSPACE 3.0 serves as a test bed for future living spaces. Bill
Gates' private house and Steven Spielberg's Minority Report paved
in relatively shy and cautious steps the road before us, now it is
time for deep implementation.*

protoSPACE 3.0
_Hyperbody 2010

3.2 *From Static to Proactive*

The second paradigm shift leading architecture towards new horizons is the step from static to interactive architecture. Exactly the same prerequisite that allows for customized CNC production also allows for dynamic behaviour of the constructs. Once the building components possess their unique numbers, once they are tagged, they can be addressed as individuals. When the individual components are continually addressed in a streaming mode in real time, and when the building components are capable of making moves, then that component may be said to be responsive, adaptive.

From responsiveness to interaction is another step. Responding to incoming information is based on information streaming in one direction from the sender to the receiver, then the receiver responding back to the sender. But this is still far from the bi-directional dialogue that characterizes the interactivity paradigm. To have interactivity, the receiver must send back new information; it must process the received information and send it back in a slightly adjusted form. Some parameters must have changed. A dialogue is a two-way communication in which each actor is somewhat changed after having sent back its response. From ear to brain to mouth; listen, think and speak: so perfectly normal for humans; so complex for machines. But small Arduino circuits are currently being developed that can actually behave as relatively dumb actors. On a local scale they receive, they process, they send signals. When these small and locally intelligent processors are built into building components, these components can then be designed as to act and react. The jump from responsive and adaptive to the proactive can then be made. Smart building components can be provided with algorithms that allow for real time behaviour, even when there has not been an explicit demand from any human for them to respond to. Thus buildings may start to act for themselves; they may start to propose changes and thereby start a dialogue with their users. The coming decade will show accelerating development from the static through the interactive towards the proactive. Only when information architects band together and gain control over the new paradigms of interactivity and proactivity, only when they include their fascination for interactivity and proactivity in their designs, and only when they develop the necessary skills to implement interactivity and proactivity in their BIMs and in their CNC-produced building components, only then can the modern information architect claim responsibility for the fascinating field of augmented architectural working space.

3.3 *Interacting Populations*

After one understands both paradigm shifts, one shift from standard to nonstandard, the other from static to proactive, it is then feasible to discuss the concept of interacting populations in the discipline of architecture. Since I have developed my buildings as information processing vehicles, it should be immediately obvious that these vehicles are not isolated objects, but are receiving and transmitting information to other such information processing systems as well, to other instrumental bodies. Just as the totality of cars on the motorway form a population of interacting mobile vehicles, these input-output (IO) instrumental bodies form a global population of interacting bodies and interacting species. Swarm behaviour forms the basis for describing and scripting the behaviour of such IO populations. The links between the IO vehicles are established locally through senders and transmitters, and globally networked through the Internet. Their behaviour is subject to local constraints (forces from within) and global constraints (forces from outside the system). What do the IO vehicles tell each other, what sort of information do they send, what information do they narrowcast?

My first truly interactive structure was the Saltwater Pavilion, built in 1997. A weather station positioned in the North Sea informed the computer running Max MSP, feeding the raw data from the weather station and in turn informing a mixing table to produce unique MIDI numbers in real time. The MIDI numbers drove the interior lights and sounds, refreshing the *massage* of light and sound 20 times per minute. The public could interact with this dynamic environment using a sensor board, pushing and pulling lights and sounds towards the extremes of the interior space. Interactive experience and architecture were both designed from scratch with similar budgets and at the same scale. In much the same way that we successfully fused art and architecture by assigning equivalent budgets and working space to both the art and the architecture, we applied this radical form of equivalent collaboration to the fusion of architecture with interaction truly a first in the history of architecture. The integration of a light-and-sound environment in architecture had been achieved before, as, for example, in the Philips Pavilion at the 1958 World Expo in Brussels, but that program was passively consumed, while the Saltwater Pavilion is a participatory environment.

Suppose we now have a swarm of water pavilions, all placed on different locations around the globe, all exchanging information with each other, with their local environment, with their local users, and also obedient to their global directives. That would then establish a hive-mind of intelligent self-aware buildings. That is the broader context I am seeking with the concept of proactivity. All IO members of the swarm would feed on data produced by other IO vehicles, all would behave in real time, all would tell the others about their behavior, and all would be self-learning entities. Self-learning capacity will only arise if the IO bodies continuously communicate with their peers as part of a dynamic swarm. Then they can begin building a body of knowledge as does the human species. It is easy to see that the human mind would be completely helpless and uninformed if it did not communicate with its peers. The human body of knowledge is not embodied in one brain; only the global hive of all connected brains has the total information and is thus able to evolve. It will be much the same with IO bodies. Their brains will feed on meaningful data from the Internet and other wireless transmitted semantic signals that they need for their metabolic operations.

3.4 Cars Are Actors

Keeping yourself in an upright position is a precarious balancing act. If you have ever tried running with your eyes closed, you know that you are bound to deviate from a straight path; you immediately start wobbling and become unsure how to proceed. You are soon lost in space. By keeping your eyes open, however, you are continually up-

CARS AND BUILDINGS ARE ACTORS

_japanwallspapers.blogspot.com

dated via your eyes on information about the path, and thus are able to respond continuously to the incoming data, able to tell your brain to send signals to your muscles to balance your body. This is how swarm behaviour works; this is how birds adjust their trajectories in the swarms; this is how cars flock on motorways as well.

Thus cars must be seen as actors on the motorway. By analysing their flocking behaviour one can see that it is the car that is responding, that the *car* uses the driver to execute the response. It is not the driver but the system – that is, the car including the driver – that makes the decisions. The car is an intelligent agent, an actor playing the rules of the motorway game. In streaming fashion the car is informed by the signs and the lines on and along the motorway, by signals from other cars, by radio signals caught by its antenna, and above all by continually measuring distance, speed and direction of neighbouring cars. This is an ongoing computational process. Even when the flock of cars comes to a complete standstill in a traffic jam the same intelligent operations are still active. The car is still measuring, still being informed, perhaps mostly by radio signals in this case. Even the car that is stopped in the traffic jam is a still a process being executed.

This notion is important for understanding future paragraphs where I focus on the behaviour of building components being actors in the building body. The car as a participant in the motorway system is not only receiving and processing, but also sending signals to its immediate neighbours. The car blinks its lights when turning left or right, it lights up its taillights when braking to slow down. In the dark, it is even more obvious how the motorway system works: only the signs lighting up and blinking signals lead the cars, there is no landscape left to distract the car body. Driving a car at night is like flying an airplane. Planes fly through virtual corridors, visualized by 3d software as a virtual tunnel with boundaries to stay within. Signals from clash-detection software will alert the plane if it deviates from its proper course. These advanced yet relatively simple techniques are now embedded in modern cars as well. The car reads the signs on the road, sends information to the steering mechanism, and at the same time informs the driver via signals and visuals.

It is by the social technique of empathy that I describe the motorway system in such a manner. It is this same empathic technique that I then apply to the informed building body system to describe how it works in real time, and how we can take advantage of this new awareness for the development of programmable building bodies. Now what processes does the car go through, what does it do with the incoming information? Let's assume that I am looking at modern cars in which hundreds of small computers are embedded to ensure the safe behaviour of the car. Thus I don't need to give the driver all of the credit for the proper response to incoming signals. Internally there is a complex of connected systems at work to validate the incoming data. When a car gets too close to another car in front of it, it diminishes its speed. When the car notices a continuous line at one side and the car shows an inclination to cross that line, the steering wheel adjusts the direction of the car, if only by a fraction of a degree. The car, in cooperation with the driver, continually fine-tunes its direction on the basis of incoming signals, just as the human body keeps itself upright and finds its direction along a straight path. Validating incoming data basically means that the incoming data, in the form of numbers, are compared to the bandwidth of allowed numbers. If the incoming value is higher or lower than the allowed value, then it is considered out-of-range and the vehicle is instructed to take action. First an out-of-range signal is sent to the steering installation to make a minor correction. It should be unnecessary to say that this is a delicate and responsive processing system. It rules over life and death. But just imagine that if you change the rotational angle of the steering wheel only a fraction of a degree yourself, you would quickly deviate from the proper path and within seconds would crash. It is amazing how subtly humans are able to operate the car to keep it on the right track. But from our empathic point of view it is similarly amazing how the car itself, by receiving wireless information, can self-correct and perform these subtle continuous corrections. The car flourishes in a flock of interacting populations of different types of cars that are interacting with their internal drivers and the external motorway system. The car has become a 'living' complex adaptive system to be admired and to serve as an ideal subject with which to investigate evolution at work.

3.5 Buildings Are Actors

Think of the behaviour of buildings as coming from members of a flock, informed actors in a swarm. What sort of information comes in, how is it processed, and what information does it spit out? How does it behave in the context of the city? Think of buildings as they are built today in the developed countries, including their cabling, wiring, piping and plumbing, including their sense organs and wireless waves. Although the infrastructure makes up at least one-third of the building budget, the building installation is the most ignored part of the building design, which is understandable as designers usually have no power to control the infrastructure in the same way that

031 NSA MUSCLE

Since 2000, ONL and Hyperbody have been busy exploring the architectural potential of programmable actuators for interactive installations and eventually for completely interactive buildings. The existence of hydraulic and electronic pistons was known, but not many actuators migrated to built structures. I had the ambition to build something like Trans-Ports before the year 2005, since I already possessed the necessary technology to build it physically at the time. But I needed a client. In 2003 I was invited to design and build an installation for the 'Nonstandard Architecture' (NSA) exhibition in the Centre Pompidou in Paris, France. I found out that Festo AG produces industrial programmable muscles, flexible tubes that become longer or shorter depending on the air pressure pumped into them. I immediately saw the potential of using Festo muscles in an interactive installation, in the project that I named the NSA Muscle. The pressurized muscles take tension forces, which must be counterbalanced by structural components that can take pressure loads. Thus I imagined an inflatable balloon wrapped in a diagrid network of connected muscles. The 72 muscles are programmed to behave as 72 individual members of a swarm. Each muscle is individually informed by the brains modelled in Virtools, via 72 corresponding valves, to shrink or to expand, but not without affecting the configurations of their neighbours. Areas of contraction and areas of expansion made the NSA Muscle dance on the exhibition floor, the muscular body has been seen to rotate, hop and crawl. Sensors on the exterior nodes can be touched by the public to produce an extra layer of information for the body to respond to. The NSA Muscle is programmed to have its own cyclic metabolism, but to respond immediately to external impulses as well. The result of the various interacting layers of the programming is a behaviour that is sensitive and slightly unpredictable, only controllable to a certain degree, according to the principles of a multi-valued fuzzy logic.

INTERIOR NSA MUSCLE CENTRE POMPIDOU PARIS

_ONL [Oosterhuis_Lénárd]
2002 / Hyperbody /
photo Kas Oosterhuis

032 protoWALL

During the years following the NSA Muscle project, Festo AG and Hyperbody agreed to cooperate on educational research projects. Hyperbody developed an experimental 'hands-on' studio for interactive architecture in the BSc 6 programme of the Faculty of Architecture at Delft University of Technology. Each semester a group of 12 students would design, build and play an interactive installation. Thus the Muscle Reconfigured was built in 2004, and subsequently the Interactive Tower (2005), the Muscle Body (2005), the Bamboostic installation (2006), the Interactive Façade (2007) and the Disappearing Entrance (2008). In 2009 the cooperation culminated in the Festo Interactive Wall project. Festo had already developed their Finray structure, which is a wing-like shape that is moved by a Festo muscle. Shrinking or expanding the muscle pulls or pushes the wing in either direction. Six wings in a row make up the Festo Interactive Wall, which Hyperbody refers to as the protoWALL. Hyperbody wrote the program for the streaming interaction, designed the LED light pattern, and assembled the active components into the swinging structure. Sensors are built in the feet of the wings; passers-by trigger the sensors, causing the corresponding part of the protoWALL to respond immediately. As people pass by, a gentle wave resembling a soft turbulence travels through the structure. The protoWALL responds to more people simultaneously, which makes the movements unpredictable in their detailed movements, and thus intriguing to watch. From the simple rules a complex behaviour is generated. As with earlier interaction projects the structures are designed to behave according to a cyclic metabolic program, and designed to be open to external impulses as well. The logic of protoWALL is a generic form of logic that is applicable to all possible building components.

INTERACTIVE WALL
_Hyperbody 2009 / Festo AG /
photo Walter Fogel

they control the geometry and the materialization of their designs. However, designers should pay more attention to this infrastructure, especially since buildings are becoming smarter and the infrastructure budgets are rising higher and higher. The building body feeds on information of many kinds. Hooked onto the infrastructural system of the city, the building body reads many wireless signals. It inhales information, some comes in digital format, and others (such as water, gas and people) come in analogue format.

By applying the principle of empathy, we see that 'people' is just another form of data from the point of view of the building body. People are selectively admitted by the building body to give character to its existence. People are the carriers of information, the translators of ephemeral information into a physical change in the building body. People effectuate changes such as switching on the lights, opening the door, plugging into the Internet.

The door is essentially a switch in the building system. When a door is open, air travels from one room to the other so that the internal conditions and hence the performance of the building changes. The performance is felt by people, and they might act by closing the door/switch again. Thus people and buildings cooperate in the functioning of the building. People operate and interact, but it is the building itself that interacts systemically with the other members of the city swarm. Using incoming data, the building body continually adjusts its internal condition. Although unlike cars it does not move along the ground, still it does change the interior temperature, the relative humidity, the amount of direct sunlight.

The building body feeds on electricity, gas and water. The electricity could be generated by photovoltaic cells that are wrapped along the skin of the building's body, or by a series of smaller wind turbines along its external edges, where the speed of the wind is naturally accelerated.

The city contains a mix of many building types, all acting as individual information-processing members of their flock, all flocks interacting with the other flocks of other typologies, all of them connected to a central nervous and lymphatic supply and waste removal system. All the members of the city swarm follow the simple rules set by the urban designers, and as imposed by their own individual feature designers, and eventually they make up the complexity of the city as a whole. The buildings are the biggest actors in the city system, structuring the movements of the inhabitants. In this way of looking at the built environment, the inhabitants only assist in the behaviour of the buildings; the people operate on parts of the buildings by supplying parameters that are read, heard or seen by the buildings in real time. In a speeded-up movie of the cityscape the people and cars move so fast that they become almost invisible shadows, while the buildings themselves seem to make their changes at normal speed.

3.6 What Is Interactive Architecture?

What exactly is interactive architecture? Let me first clarify what it is *not*. Interactive architecture (iA) is *not* simply a structure designed to be responsive or adaptive to changing circumstances. It is not a response to pushing a button, as when switching on

**INTERACTIVE
ENTRANCE**
_Hyperbody 2008

the lights. It is much more than that; it is based on the concept
that bi-directional communication requires two active parties.
Communication between two people is interactive naturally; they
each listen (the input), think (the processing part) and talk (the
output). But iA is not about communication between people; it is
defined first as the art of building relationships between tagged
built components, and second, in the art of building relationships
between people and the built components. It is the art of building
bi-directional relationships in real time. In our approach, all built
components are seen as input-processing output (IPO) devices.
The theory of iA includes both passive and active IPO systems.

Let me clarify this once more with the classic example of the
door. As I have described above, the door in the building functions as a switch. It is either open or closed. When we add the
lock to the door, it is then either locked or unlocked and the one
who has the key is the only one authorized to lock and unlock
the door. In the building the door functions as a semi-permeable
membrane for the two spaces A and B on either side of the door.
The door allows people or goods to come in or go out. What about
the processing part of the IPO procedure? The door can be said to
process people (including the bags that are carried as backpacked
information by the people), to process the air flow, the dust
particles, the transport of aromatic molecules. When the door is
opened the two systems on either side will find a new equilibrium
with respect to number of people, goods, light, temperature, data.
An actively computing door processes by quantifying what passes
through the opening.

In iA it unfolds exactly like that. The iA software counts whatever changes occur in the positions, configurations and other possible characteristics of any IPO object. Each object that is defined
in Hyperbody's protoSPACE software behaves in real time to keep

track of changes of their neighbouring objects. Each object is then an IPO machine, an agent communicating with other agents, like birds communicating with other birds in the swarm. Understanding iA is not possible without having understood and adopted the rules of nonstandard architecture (NSA) in the design process. As explained in the second chapter, NSA implies that all constituent components of a built construct are unique. They each have a unique number, position and shape. If two components are the same then it is pure coincidence and *not* simplifying the structure per se. In the design process and in the mass customized file-to-factory production process all components are addressed individually. No longer is repetition the basis for production and hence design. Repetition is no longer beautiful. In NSA the uniqueness of the components is what is felt to be natural, logical and beautiful. Once all building components have a unique number, when they are tagged to be addressed in real time, the components then can instantly change their mutual positions. Floors can become protoDECKs, walls can become Interactive Walls, and building bodies can become Muscle Bodies. Having designed and built a dozen interactive prototypes, Hyperbody knows how realistic it is to think of a building as consisting of interacting populations of building components being informed in real time to either act slowly as if frozen to death or to act in an excited way in order to enjoy a dialogue with their users.

MUSCLE BODY
_Hyperbody 2005

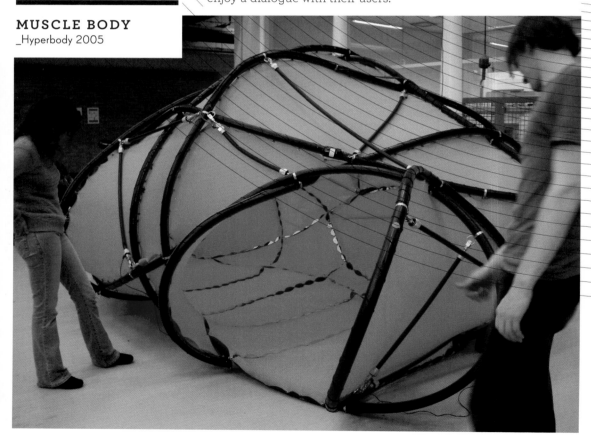

3.7 Proactivity

Despite all the achievements of nonstandard architecture in the dynamic design process, the built NSA product is still static just as is the modernist building that is based on repetitive mass production. The door I took as an example is, in static architecture, usually operated by a human, although some doors are automatic. But the currently unfolding IT revolution is significantly affecting the operation of doors and locks. Doors will become self-aware IPO devices following their own local behavioural instructions, while at the same time listening to top-down authorized commands. Soon these doors will lock and unlock, open and close as they wish, and if you are authorized to do so they will also open when *you* wish them to open. Doors will themselves become aware of changing circumstances, and they will act accordingly without having to receive an additional instruction to act. Doors will become active building components, and so will each of the thousands of individual components that make up the overall built construct. Once electronics sneak into the building components the logical first step is that the doors will respond deliberately, based on a complex evaluation of many impulses. After that has been achieved, the next logical step is that they will become proactive. They will start proposing changes themselves. Nothing to get worried about, however, humans will still co-evolve just like they co-evolved with dogs and other domesticated life forms. Proactive doors will become domesticated as well. Instead of being fearful of so much action, you will like it because of its liveliness.

To summarize, iA is not just responsive and adaptive, it is also pro-active. Building components that are iA-tuned are capable of a wealth of subtle actions; they constantly propose new configurations in real time, sometimes unnoticeably slowly, sometimes faster than you can move your eyes and faster than you can think. In iA software the active behaviour is built deep into the scripted code of the design, into its own DNA structure. Each component calculates its new input in real time, many times per second, and produces its new output behaviour, thereby continuously changing the state it is in. This ever-changing state acts as new input into the IPO system of other components and so on and so on, as actors in the interacting populations. The entire set of thousands of active components makes up the complex adaptive system (CAS) of the building.

The art of designing interactive architecture then is defined as the art of conceptualizing the CAS and the art of imposing style on the active building materials. A designer must keep in mind the fact that many of the constituent components are programmable actuators. This is a paradigm shift for the creative designer, as the architect thus becomes an information architect. The information architect sculpts data, designs the flow of information and constructs the IPO components to selectively transmit, absorb, transform or simply bounce back the information flow. My objective is to always make sure that iA is perceived as beautiful, that it not be experienced as merely a technical achievement. Can iA compete with conservative architecture as we have learned to

NSA MUSCLE CENTRE POMPIDOU PARIS

_ONL [Oosterhuis_Lénárd] 2002
/ Hyperbody /
photo Kas Oosterhuis

48° 51' 38'' N
2° 21' 08'' E

appreciate it as meaningful, relevant and beautiful? My personal view is that iA naturally deals with beauty since objects in (slow) motion always get more attention than static objects. People relate emotionally more easily to dynamic structures than to static ones. It simply is more fun to watch live painting than to watch the paint dry. And when we train ourselves to not be satisfied with the initial fascinating fact that a building moves, when we train ourselves to be concerned about *how* it moves, when we focus, as we should, on the fashionable and stylish aspects of the iA design concepts, then the age of interactive architecture will have arrived, then information architects will be respected designers of proactive structures.

3.8 There Is Only a Window When You Need One

Previously we discussed the different modes of the iWEB, the spaceship that can alternately be art or architecture, and thus is both art *and* architecture. The difference between the two was created by a giant door mounted on hinges. The iWEB building itself is a static structure, the door is positioned at a fixed place and there are only two different modes. However, our Trans-Ports project showed that a building need not be restricted to two modes. Trans-Ports can be in education mode, in lounge mode, in lecture mode, in research mode, in playtime mode, in nightclub mode. The space itself is envisioned to be able to change shape and content in real time. Trans-Ports is a multimodal design concept, physically actualized as a structure with a telescopic structure and a flexible skin. The skin material of Trans-Ports always remains the same skin, while the structure is equipped with the same set of electronic pistons but in different physical configurations. The built structure itself does not change in principle, but it has the built-in capacity to behave, to move its skeleton, to stretch its skin. Now imagine that the door is not hung from hinges but is thought of as a responsive, adaptive and proactive specialization of the skin. Suppose that the skin could change its physical properties at any place on the surface, just by reprogramming its constituting components.

The interactive prototype Hyperbody that students built during the spring semester of 2008 carries out the idea of an interactive entrance, a semi-permeable wall through which one would wade rather than enter through a specific portal. There would only be an opening in the wall when someone stood close enough to it and the wall would open only there. The entrance would not have a fixed position; it could be any place along that wall. You might compare it to the ground floor façade of a large building with thousands of small automatic doors, all responsive to sensors. The only area that would open for you would be the area of actuating components that you were closest to and were authorized to open. Thus a building façade would become something you could wade through; there would be no hierarchy in the floor plan. This sounds like a speculative thought experiment, but it is perfectly possible to do today with existing technology. My students are typically able to design and build such a façade in six to eight weeks, even without previous knowledge of interaction design. It

ADAPTIVE FACADE
_ONL [Oosterhuis_Lénárd] 2004

is that simple, only needing a switch inside your brain to look at things differently.

For the process of actually making the prototype, each actuating component must be embedded with a small processor to read an RFID tag, then process the information and act accordingly. When the door knows you and trusts you, when your data matches its own data, it will let you in. When the door does not know you, you will not have the privilege of wading through the building wall, and you will have to take the lane for unidentified guests. Perhaps there could be a website where you could introduce yourself, get your tag, and get authorized to open the doors. Scary? Not at all. Something similar already happens when you check-in for your flight online and get yourself authorized to skip the check-in desk. The tag may take the form of a barcode in this instance, but much more sophisticated devices are also available on the market that can be woven into your clothes so that you do not have to show the printed version. The desk would automatically recognize your signal and let you through. Obstructive barriers would thus be dissolved, but there's nothing to be afraid of, as was suggested between the lines in the movie *Minority Report*. When watching *Minority Report* I realized that I could do exactly the same thing with knowledge developed during the first decades of existence of ONL/Hyperbody. Tagging yourself with wearable miniature IPO dust would be more reliable than any other form of identification, much friendlier than oversized passports and identification cards. Identity may even become integrated with fashion and become a matter of dressing, a daily routine.

Now suppose that you not only imagine interacting with doors but with a complete building envelope, and with all the flexible interior separation walls, and with the floors and ceilings too. These building components can be embedded in much the same way with intelligent agents and actuators that can interact with your personal profile. Thus any façade can become a truly interactive envelope, opening and closing for light and fresh air wherever, whenever and whoever may want it – you, by yourself, or the space you are in, by itself. There would only be a window when there was a locally expressed need for one.

033 DIGITAL PAVILION IMMEDIATE DESIGN

In the conceptual phase of the design for the Digital Pavilion in Seoul, commissioned by a large South-Korean interior design firm, I decided to use three-dimensional Voronoi cells to form the basis for the spatial layout. The uniqueness of the design process is that the point cloud of reference points for the three-dimensional Voronoi calculation is created 'on the fly'. I asked Hyperbody PHD candidate Christian Friedrich to customize the immediate design tool for the Digital Pavilion project, the tool that he had developed earlier for his brilliant thesis project at Hyperbody. Designing on the fly comes down to making design decisions while being active inside the running design game. The Virtools game development platform is used to help the designer place the points of the point cloud while navigating through the space. These points are then seen as the centre points of the three-dimensional Voronoi, and thereafter the edgy soap bubble structure is built up using those points. Points can be added and deleted whenever desired while designing, while being in the game. Thus a spectacular immediate aspect is added to the repertoire of the information architect, the digitally enhanced designer. Designing on the fly is as close to their intuition as designers can get. Any intuitive act or gesture has an immediate effect on the three-dimensional world one is shaping. Every modification can be scrutinized from all angles since one can navigate freely in one's own personal design universe. For practical design reasons the three-dimensional Voronoi structure, which is in principle without boundaries, is cut off where the floors of the existing building end. By the end of the streaming design exercise one continuous three-dimensional structure covered the three floors of the exhibition space, building up a virtual spatial connection between the otherwise separate floors. In the augmented world on the PDAs and the goggles the public experiences the continuity of the three-dimensional Voronoi structure penetrating the floors.

DESIGN ON THE FLY DIGITAL PAVILION SEOUL

_ONL [Oosterhuis_Lénárd] 2007 / Hyperbody Christian Friedrich

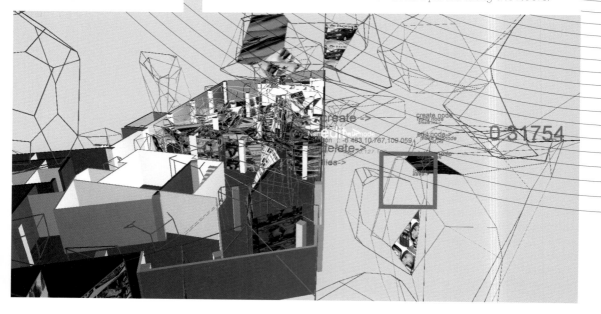

034 DIGITAL PAVILION AUGMENTED REALITY

INTER-ACTIVE STRUCTURE DIGITAL PAVILION SEOUL

_ONL [Oosterhuis_Lénárd] 2007

On entering the exhibition space the public is initiated; each person is tagged so they are identifiable by their friends and by the exhibition objects alike. Imagine that the exhibition objects know your profile. These smart exhibition objects adjust the level of information that is transmitted to you on the basis of the settings you have uploaded to your profile. Part of your profile must be made before you come to the exhibition site via the Digital Pavilion website. The other part is built up while you walk through the exhibition itself. For instance, if you look longer at a certain object than at other objects, the tiny brains of that object understand that you are interested and will add this fact to your profile. A next object reads this and adjusts the nature of the information accordingly, by showing another image, or by telling a different story, more closely related to your own interests. Another important feature of the interactive exhibition design is the real time behaviour of the exhibition structure itself. Sensors are embedded in the electronic pistons so they know when a person wishes to pass. A structurally dense part may open up to provide a passage when someone with the proper profile comes close enough. 'There is only a passage when you need one.' Part of the exhibition floor is designed to be executed using electronic pistons for all its structural members. The public would feel as if caught in a dense structural three-dimensional Voronoi web, only getting the chance to exit when triggering the right combination of sensors. Escaping from the web space is designed be a real time game that the public will play within the physical exhibition, in a deep merge between the real and the virtual, in a bodily version of augmented reality.

3.9 Versatile Time Zones

Let us perform another thought experiment. As are many other travellers, I am often disturbed by the different time zones, especially because of their irrational simplified structure. The time zones simply do not match up with high resolution reality. Is there another solution possible to account for the passage of time, other than the low resolution division of the world into 24 time zones? Dividing the world into just two dozen time zones is just as primitive as is a picture of 5 by 5 or 25 pixels to depict the world. The nonstandard approach (NSA), since it deals with the notion of the mathematically infinite, would naturally lead logically to an unlimited number of time zones. The NSA approach would facilitate a perfectly smooth transition from one spot on earth to another, without the rude one-hour jumps. Time would be stretched along with your own movement over the surface of the earth. Time would be real time. You can imagine having an atomic clock in your cell phone indicating the exact time on that very place where you are – just there, just then.

When you travelled in the same direction as the rotation of the earth, your watch would tick slightly slower, because you would be going faster than the flow of time. When you stop for a moment for a stoplight, the watch would slow down to the general speed of the rotation of the earth again. And when you were travelling in the opposite direction your clock would speed up to compensate for the loss of time. (Remember that the USA is always six to nine hours behind Central European Time, while China is well ahead of that.) Now instead of resetting your clock manually when arriving

24 TIME ZONES
_Geoscience Australia

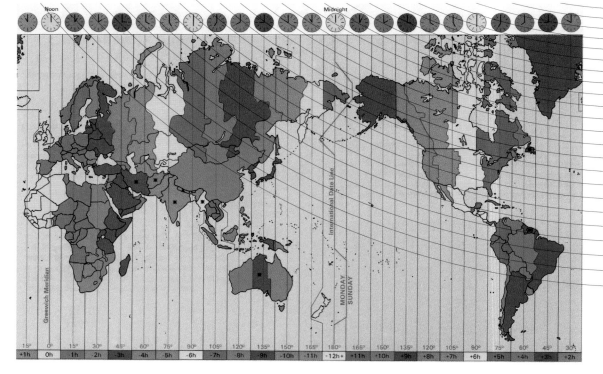

in the USA from Europe, your clock would have done that for you during your trip in a high-resolution streaming fashion. It would keep track of the changes in real time, many times per second. That real time clock would need to be tagged to communicate its position on earth, and it would need to send, process and receive information with other tagged clocks (a swarm of satellites) in real time. The complete network of tagged watches and clocks would take care of the worldwide distribution of the proper time, as high-resolution as is technically possible, with no more time lags, paving the way for smooth (variomatic) awareness of time. Your variomatic clock would no longer be an old-school mechanical watch; it would be a computer, keeping track of the real time in real time.

Just imagine the effect it would have on the daily lives of people. If we abandoned the low-resolution division into 24 time zones, everyone and everything would have its own personal time. When making phone calls one would be able to see the exact time difference from the other end. And with devices interacting with each other, there would be a *delta t* keeping track of each individual time position. This thought experiment of versatile time zones could only become reality if everything was tagged and had a small processor embedded, exactly the condition I foresee for all building components in nonstandard and interactive architecture. The obvious advantage is that, just as the complexity of nonstandard architecture will feel natural and comfortable, having the precise time without ever having to adjust your watch will also feel natural and comfortable. We will live closer to the unfolding computation of nature, which will no longer be brutally cut into low-resolution chunks of time. That nature is, when all is said and done, a computation has been argued by Stephen Wolfram in his prophetic book *A New Kind of Science*. He proposes that nature be understood as a complex set of executing cellular automata, performing probably billions of operations per second. Nature, then, is one big transaction space, negotiating vast amounts of data.

3.10 The Actuator

One more thought experiment, this time not on stretching time but on stretching the physical structure of a high-rise tower. This thought experiment explores the potential of programmable architecture. Imagine a one-mile-high tower – not feasible unless we apply the new technology of programmable building components. As explained before, we can apply the technique of programming embedded actuators to bring more excitement into the built structure as it changes shape in real time. Moreover, a programmable building can also be programmed to dynamically freeze into an extremely motionless crystal. Let's investigate in further detail this extreme end of the spectrum of possibilities of programmable architecture. While there is no bandwidth for static architecture since it is fixed to one particular configuration, the bandwidth of the behaviour of buildings with actuators may range from almost zero to almost endless: zero being the completely frozen situation; endless being the maximum amount of movements that is mechanically and electronically feasible.

ONE MILE HIGH TOWER JEDDAH

_SOM /

photomontage Zohair Alghamdi

SKYSCRAPERCITY.COM/SAUDIA ARABIA-JEDDAH/PHOTO BY SAUDI GUY
RENDER-IMAGINATION/THE MILE TOWER,1600M

So the position of one on a logarithmic scale of proactivity represents the static configuration of the inert buildings you see around you. The static reality means that conservative high-rise buildings will swing from side to side with a substantial amount of sway. The sway of the late World Trade Center towers was measured to be more than 1 m. A sway as large as 1 m is definitely not pleasant; one could easily develop seasickness. If it were possible to avoid sway caused by the stronger winds higher up in the air, then it would be possible to build much higher.

The height of buildings has always been constrained by what is technically possible. The elevator paved the road for the first generation of high-rises, innovations in steel and concrete structures stretched the upper limits to 800 m as recently seen in Dubai, the United Arab Emirates, by the high-rise structure renamed the Burj Al Khalifa in 2010 (since the ruler of Abu Dhabi, Al Khalifa paid the debts of Dubai). Frank Lloyd Wright wanted to build a One Mile High Tower, and he even made a sketch of it – a large foot that diminished in size towards the top like a vertically stretched pyramid. Basically all high-rise towers, including the Burj Al Khalifa, follow more or less that conceptual idea.

Recently a proposal was published for a one-mile-high tower in Saudi Arabia, the Jeddah Tower by Adrian Smith + Gordon Gill Architecture. Here is a quote from the designers:

Architecture and engineering have traditionally treated structure as static – the building frame was constructed to be strong and heavy enough to resist all anticipated loads. The Mile High Tower proposes a lighter, dynamic structural system that actively responds to forces placed upon it. Controlled by wind detecting sensors, stabilizing aileron-like fins run the length of the tower frame and modulate their position to control resonant motion and building drift.

To me, this accurately describes the kind of architecture society is heading for in the coming decades. Buildings will become lighter and structural systems will respond to changing loads. Such a one-mile-high-tower could theoretically be frozen into a perfectly upright position, without any deviation from its upright position as caused by winds or other disturbances. However, the Jeddah Tower still follows the old aesthetic of the super high-rise; it is still basically a stretched pyramid. I would rather have opted for a tower that increases in size towards the higher levels, perhaps taking advantage of the strong winds higher up in the air by capturing the power with wind turbines, meanwhile securing its uprightness by a substantially dense diagrid web of actuators on the exterior load-bearing skin. I would have also opted for a swarm of actuators to ensure that if one or more actuators failed the others would take over that function, emulating a robust network of thousands of cooperating players, like birds in a swarm.

4.

> *Evolve That Body*

*the building body
is a personal
universe
living inside
evolution*

4.1 My Personal Brain

My brain is connected to the other six billion brains of the world in a most complex way. I am connected to the other brains through images, sounds, smells, words, radio waves, light and motion. Sounds come into my brain and are transmitted outward through language, music, noise. I am linked to all the brains on earth by six degrees of separation, on average, as was originally suggested by the Hungarian author Frigyes Karinthy in his 1929 book *Everything Is Different*. My brain could not possibly function if not connected with thousands of other brains. It is fair to say that a single isolated brain has never existed. Brains have evolved in connection with millions of other brains. It is only by their connectivity that they have been able to develop from primitive amoeba stages to the stage of development we are now living in. I would not know anything – no language, no knowledge – if I had not been part of such a dense network of connected brains. I also assume that our brains operate like birds in a swarm, connecting to their neighbouring brains in real time, importing data, processing information and producing output data again to be absorbed by their peers. That is a single degree of separation, similar to a single degree of connectivity. Within six degrees of connectivity I have access to all other brains. I am living *inside evolution* in an extensively shared environment.

The connectivity is not only between the members of the species of people, but also between people and the objects that surround them that have degrees of separation/connectivity as well. For example, the styling of products like cars also relates to other designs in a number of degrees of connectivity. Almost everything somehow relates to something else, either from the same species, or via features that are similar but from different species. Evolving nature includes product life, that is, the evolution of paper clips, pottery, furniture, computers, cell phones, cars, houses, motorways, airplanes, cities, reclaimed land, satellites, space stations – all of that is product life.

Links and degrees of separation/connectivity of one's own brain to other people, to texts, images and websites are mirrored in the software Personal Brain, developed by The Brain Technologies starting in 1988. I used Personal Brain in my inaugural speech at Delft University of Technology in 2001. I showed images by navigating through my own personal brain, while my virtual friend Marlon (see www.haptek.com) asked me questions. That inaugural speech set the tone for Hyperbody's subsequent research on swarm behaviour, about which a comprehensive book on Hyperbody's first decade of interactive architecture will be released by the end of 2010.

4.2 My Personal Design Point Cloud

My personal design universe consists of interacting populations of groups of points in space, wirelessly connected by force fields that are aware of themselves, communicating with their immediate neighbours, and subject to the imposing forces of powerlines. My design universe includes interacting point clouds, in which each point behaves as if it is the centre of the world, even though it is just 'somewhere', as our Earth is just somewhere in the Milky Way. The centre of your Universe is where you are. All living beings and all artefacts feel and act as if they are the centre of the world, since they cannot help but think locally. Each point is an actor, always busy measuring and adjusting its position in relation to its peers. Each point is an actuator, triggering the execution of its internal program. Each point is an IPO, a receiver, processor and sender in one. Each point of my personal design point cloud displays behaviour, it has character and style. Each point of the point cloud is a microscopic instrument to be played, a game to be unfolded. Each point is a running process, a cellular automaton.

Hans L.C. Jaffé

BROADWAY BOOGIE WOOGIE PIET MONDRIAN 1942

_Mondriaan, 1985
Hans LC Jaffé
publisher Harry N Abrams
New York

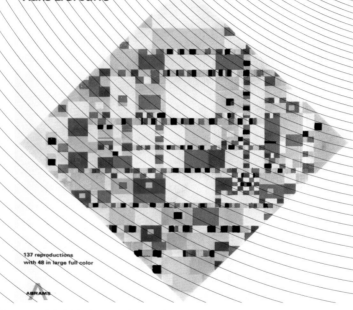

137 reproductions
with 48 in large full-color

ABRAMS

035 MONDRIAN'S PERSONAL UNIVERSE

Mondrian's personal universe had no end and no beginning, his imaginary universe continued beyond the borders of his paintings. In Mondrian's universe all of the components - the stripes, the colour fields, the coloured squares on the white canvas - were imagined by him to be in motion. What Mondrian did while painting is to keep the components in motion as long as possible. Every day he would change the positions of the components on his canvas. Thus Broadway Boogie Woogie is an instance of an otherwise dynamic universe. In his studio Mondrian surrounded himself with many such instances; he virtually lived inside his universe. The painting can be seen as a local densification of an endless universe, where the actors, that is the stripes and dots, are attracted and organized by the personal brain of Mondrian. The local and temporary crystallization of that personal universe is then again revitalized by the observers of the painting in the museum, recreating such a universe while retrieving the visual data.

036 FRANK STELLA'S PAINTING INTO ARCHITECTURE

FRANK STELLA CYTHOLOGY AT SYNTHETIC DIMENSION ZONNEHOF AMERS- FOORT 1991
_photo Kas Oosterhuis

Frank Stella augmented his working space by liberating the painting from the wall. Working Space is also the title of the book he wrote in 1986, relating his own work to art theory from Caravaggio via Pollock to graffiti street artists. After a minimalist period Stella created a personal universe that is polychromatic, biomorphic, enigmatic, kaleidoscopic, abstract and complex at the same time. Stella learned to apply procedural gestures, inspired by Pollock, to cover some surfaces, but he also mapped geometrical patterns on others. The importance of Stella to my own work, however, is that he exploded the flat painting into space. Ilona Lénárd and I invited Stella to exhibit one of his three-dimensional constructs from the Cones and Pillar series (1986) in the exhibition 'The Synthetic Dimension' in 1991, which we curated with Paul Coumans of Museum De Zonnehof in Amersfoort, a cute little Rietveld building. Stella's paintings became multilayered constructs, jutting into the exhibition space of the gallery. First using canvas, later working with building materials like aluminium sandwich panels that could resist the forces of being slung into space, Stella painted into architecture, in partly overlapping layers, later in the form of detached three-dimensional sculptural objects. It was Stella's ambition to have his vision realized on the scale of buildings, as he demonstrated with his pavilion design for the Groninger Museum and for the Art Museum complex in Dresden, both of which unfortunately were never realized.

As a human being I have developed radical empathy with the concept of the point cloud. I move myself into the position of the point, I mentalize that point. I have internalized the design point cloud in my mind, mapping the points spatially on the neurons of my brain; the points populate my brain. The point cloud is the initial condition from which my swarm architecture designs originate. My point cloud has no hierarchy, no centre, and the shape is always changing as in any swarm: variable, dynamic, interactive, proactive. It is a living diagram using the continuum of my brain as its habitat, connected to six billion other brains, to other volatile sets of concepts and ideas, connected to the genes of what I see around me, the genes of old and new nature alike. My point cloud is structured as a quantum building information model (qBIM), parametric in its nature, open to imposed streaming external data, deducing its internal consistency from the bi-directional relations between the actors of the point hive. Based on the continuous transaction between the points, that hive is in a state of continuous evolution, building up the critical mass needed to eventually make substantial jumps in its evolutionary development. Evolve the swarm in order to specialize the chicken from the egg.

4.3 My Personal Universe

The reason I must bring up the notion of the personal design point cloud is that the personal universe is a basic condition from which each designer starts constructing concepts. Each design originates from within an evolving and highly connected universe. Each designer incorporates a personal universe of some sort, a universe of nodes and connections, an abstract construct with the brain as a habitat, augmented with the designer's body and bodily extensions. In the Universe as it is known, there are planetary systems and galaxies, millions of them. Since it is not known what the exact nature is of what can be seen using telescopic sensory extensions, it can only be described, and by describing it, a universe inside our brains can be constructed.

The abstract universal system I have constructed within my own brain has specific qualities that most likely differ from universal constructs inside the heads of other designers. My personal universe is a system of swarming immaterial objects connected to each other by behavioural rules. My personal universe consists of actors and actuators, not of dead material circling around each other without purpose. I have trained myself to always question the existence of hard-boiled atoms, to even question the physical existence of quarks, because I know that the common picture of atoms as hard little round balls is misleadingly false. Because I know that the universal building blocks, much smaller than atoms, some of them miniscule like the Higgs particle (yet to be discovered in the large supercollider installation in Geneva), are in fact not tangible components at all. What they really are is not known, but one should not fall into the trap of using simplified, thus false pictures. Using false pictures discourages further discoveries, oversimplified and hence misguiding pictures function as show stoppers, as anchor points to temporarily hold on to, but are misleading in their nature. In my personal universal construct I assume that the reference

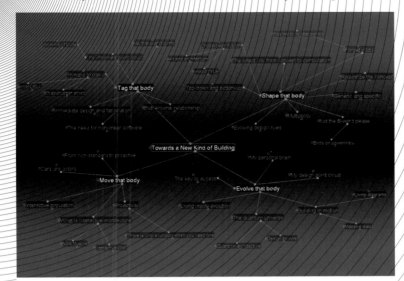

PERSONAL BRAIN OF TOWARDS A NEW KIND OF BUILDING

_thebrain.com

points are immaterial tension fields following a set of simple rules to keep distance, to attract or repel, to flock together, to have a drive in a certain direction, to behave according to swarm logic. None of these reference points are exactly the same as is also true of a flock of birds, of a school of fish, of people in a warehouse.

For me, the most challenging assumption is what the consequence would be like if the analogy to the swarm holds. Then no single quark or Higgs particle would be the same as another. They would all have an outspoken individual character within the bandwidth of genetic characteristics defining their species. As far as I know, and I have tested this idea in discussions with physicists, this kind of quantum behavioural aspect of the microcosmic world has not yet been taken into account. Questioning the quantum nature of the smallest particles leads to a series of new questions, opens up new horizons. My purpose, my not-so-hidden agenda, is to find a link between architecture and quantum science. I want architecture and design at large to be verifiable, falsifiable, intuitive and unpredictable at the same time.

4.4 Transaction Space

I became interested in the questions raised by quantum physicists after reading several essays in *Scientific American* and after reading Ayssar Arida's book *Quantum City*. Not surprisingly, Arida treats quantum as a metaphor, but since I do not much care for metaphors, I seek instead an internalized meaning of quantum. If I reject the metaphor so as to not allow myself to use false pictures, how then could I work with the notion of 'quantum' when constructing my personal design universe? Introducing the concept of swarm behaviour to explain the paradox of quantum mechanics seems to me to be an intriguing option. I know I am not an expert in the field of quantum mechanics, but somehow it works for me to think according to quantum logic. One problem that has not yet been solved in quantum mechanics is that the quantum dot has two faces, depending on how you look at it, depending on how you measure it. Perhaps the act

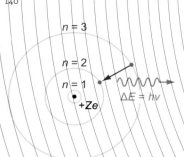

**NIELS BOHR
ATOMIC MODEL**

_wikipedia.com

of measuring imposes itself as an external factor on the quantum system, causing the system to behave differently.

Imagine two swarms of birds (obviously my favourite mental mapping device), one swarm in the air, the other swarm attracted by a power line. In both cases it is the same swarm, but drawn in a different configuration. One must realize that the birds on the power line are still swarming, but something has changed dramatically; they were informed by the long wire of the power line, which had the effect of attracting them to the wire where they neatly arranged themselves. I must assume that the birds on a wire are still in flocking mode, that they are still obeying their basic flocking rules concerning distance, speed and direction. Only the parameters driving the system have changed, some parameters even set to zero in the case of the speed parameter. So my hunch is that these two configurations are two possible faces of the same swarm.

Going back to quantum physics, my hunch is that the particle disguise and the wave disguise of quantum dots are two faces of the same quantum swarm. These two faces cannot appear simultaneously, the swarm is either on the power line or in the air. Interfering with the system by inspecting it with technical extensions of human exo-eyes such as microscopic instruments is like attracting the birds to sit on the power line. If this is indeed the case, then one should be able to model this in a dynamic parametric model, in a quantum world with real time communicating components, exchanging information, learning from each other, evolving in time, subject to external forces. If my assumption is right, then the quantum dots must be able to act and be measured while acting, if only one could work within the dynamics of the quantum system, if only one did not destroy the dynamic quantum logic by measuring it, if only one could run the system as an unfolding transaction game and look at the system from the players' perspective from within the unfolding transactions.

This argument brings the focus back to ONL's programmable projects and Hyperbody´s PhD research on designing on the fly, on designing while being inside the design game, on living inside evolution in general. Here the design process is perceived as a transaction, the buildings are acknowledged to be transaction spaces facilitating transaction between the users and their immediate environment – transactions between user and user, between component and component, between user and component.

4.5 Instances of a Quantum Universe

There are as many personal universes as there are people, as there are industrial products. All these personal universes have a certain character, sharing many generic features with each other, but also different from each other in their details. The dynamic relations and the transactions between these personal universes can exist specifically because they are slightly different. By being different, there is opportunity for information exchange. Suppose all were exactly the same, then information exchange would be completely useless. The receiver of the information could only confirm: 'yes, I agree'; 'yes, you're right'; 'yes, same with me'. After some attempts at communication these identical beings would stop exchanging information.

iLITE LIGHT ON THE MOVE
_ONL [Oosterhuis_Lénárd] 2007 / Philips / Hyperbody Dieter Vandoren

Would that not be the same on the level of atoms and quarks? Would not the system come to a complete halt if particles were indeed identical? I think this thought exercise builds a strong case for the idea that not being identical is a primary condition for dynamic systems, for exchange, for communication, for evolution at large.

Since childhood I have been intrigued by the personal universe of Mondrian. His peers had similar universes in their heads, but a slightly different and less *idiot savant* style. Together these heads filled with their personal universes formed a group, the De Stijl group, a swarm of resonating brains, out of sync with the majority of brains in that period of history, and only synchronized with each other during a short period of time. They touched upon each others' brain waves only at short intervals, and then, drawing their own conclusions, evolved in different directions, separating themselves from each other again. I feel the personal universe of Mondrian was strongly related to mine. He regarded his later paintings as a temporary crystallization of a continuous universe where everything was moving, not static. His universe must have been a world in motion, he must have seen floating horizontal and vertical bars, pulsating dots in a vast white space, not a black space as photographs and artists' impressions of the universe often suggest. He also must have recognized that these lines and dots were not copies of the same pattern, that all of them have their unique identities, and that this is exactly why they float and move about. Only when things are different is a potential energy built up that is the *sine qua non* for motion. Mondrian must have experienced himself as living inside this continuum of floating lines and coloured carpets, not looking at them, but immersed *in* them. Since he surrounded himself in his studio with exactly the same components that constitute his paintings in order to live and work inside his paintings, his universe was not only in front of him but also behind, below and above, inside and outside of himself.

Being an architect who deals with spatial realities, I am interested in how to map such a personal universe onto a three-dimensional world, instead of on a flat canvas as Mondrian did as a painter. Architect and furniture builder Gerrit Rietveld, one of Mondrian's peers, found a convincing way to develop the concept of the spatial continuum when he designed the Schröder House. Nowadays we would illustrate this concept using animation techniques, with bars and colour fields slowly travelling in endless space, changing relative distance and absolute size with variable speed, appearing and disappearing, changing direction, concentrating and deconcentrating, behaving unpredictably in every detail.

My first attempt in this direction was in Rotterdam in 1988 when I was invited by curator Evert van Straaten to make a video of the Maison Particulière for the Theo van Doesburg exhibition in Museum Boymans van Beuningen. I tried to catch that continuous universe in an animated scenario, built with then state-of-the-art computer software. The bases for the animation were moving individual components of which the Maison Particulière represented a temporary instance. I placed individual coloured components in a white three-dimensional virtual space, connected each component individually to a specified path in space, all leading towards their temporary destiny to be assembled as the Maison Particulière. I chose to create the effect of alternating implosions towards the concise configuration of the house and explosions towards individual floating elements in endless space, thus telling the story of how seemingly unconnected components can temporarily form a unified whole. Through this project I achieved for myself a deep understanding of how a personal design universe could crystallize into a three-dimensional environment. In 2007 I was asked by Philips to do an interactive installation in the international *Lights on the Move* show, and I again created, with the support of my Hyperbody staff, a dynamic system of an endlessly changing universe of light bars and light dots, triggered in intensity and speed by the presence of the visitors. I consider my design work to be primarily the design of a body in motion, as a family member of a swarm of building bodies, as a local densification of matter and concept, as an instance of an unpredictable but quantifiable quantum universe.

037 A NEW KIND OF SCIENCE

The thousand plus pages of Stephen Wolfram's book A New Kind of Science (2002) did not stop me from reading it from cover to cover. I was especially caught by his statement that nature is a computation. To prove his hypothesis Wolfram proposes the principle of computational equivalence, which states that systems found in the natural world can perform computations up to a maximal (universal) level of computational power. He claims that most systems can attain that level. Complex adaptive systems like the human brain or the global weather system in principle compute processes similar to those of a computer. Computation is a matter of input processing and output from one system to another. Consequently, most systems, nature and products alike, are computationally equivalent. Wolfram's natural physics insights resonate completely with my statement that people and building components must be seen as interacting actors. Environments at large are complex sets

STEPHEN WOLFRAM
A NEW KIND OF SCIENCE

A NEW KIND OF SCIENCE 2002

_wolframscience.com

of interacting adaptive systems, encompassing human players and players that are industrial products, including all building components. When people and building components are tagged by embedding them with tiny processors, all of them with the ability to communicate using a mutually agreed computing language, it becomes clear that natural life and product life must no longer be seen as opposites. Nature will no longer be something other than yourself, and no longer something other than the products you are surrounded by all the time. Just as nature is a computation, product life is a computation, and the relation between yourself and the products surrounding you is a computational process as well.

038 THE MEDIUM IS THE MASSAGE

Marshal McLuhan wrote his book The Medium is the Massage in 1967, as an inventory of the effects of numerous media in terms of how they knead the human sensorium (visualized in his book by graphic artist Quentin Fiore). Although I did not read the book back then and hence was not aware of the content for a long period of time, I applied a similar logic of media to the interior design of the Saltwater Pavilion. I named the upper space of the Saltwater Pavilion the Sensorium, without realizing that McLuhan used this word to indicate the complex of sensory organs including the skin of the human body. The intention of the Sensorium was exactly to create a true massage of our sense organs, with the emphasis on ears, eyes and skin. The skin would feel the water tunnel, the eyes the lightscape and the virtual reality environment, the ears the soundscape. The massage was connected to a weather station on a buoy in the North Sea in real time, measuring wave length, wind speed, percentage of salt, temperature. The programmers used these data as raw data, that is without their original meaning, to feed the PCs running MAX MSP software to translate the raw data into MIDI signals, numbers between 1 and 128. In turn the MIDI signals feed the automated sliders of a professional mixing table operating the fibreglass light optics and feed the sound synthesizing program with an updated selection from the sound samples in real time, that is 20 times per second. The public experiences a massage of light and sound and becomes receptive to more detailed information on specific water management related issues, which the client, the Dutch Ministry of Traffic and Water, wished to communicate.

THE MEDIUM IS THE MASSAGE 1967

_marshallmcluhan.com

4.6 Living Inside Evolution

Daily, I imagine the behavioural nature of the smallest components of the world around us, both the world that is usually experienced as nature and the world that is usually seen as artificial. Just look around you. If you are sitting in a room and not outside in the open, what do you see? You are completely surrounded by things, by products of some sort, smaller products and larger products. I'll bet that 95 per cent of what you see around you is made up of products composed in a surprisingly complex way. Often we take the complexity of products for granted, but personally I am

**AL NASSER
HEAD-
QUARTERS
ABU DHABI**
_ONL [Oosterhuis_Lénárd]
2007-2011

**24° 25' 12'' N
54° 26' 30'' E**

totally intrigued by the complexity of how products flock together, and even more intrigued by the complexity of organic nature. All surrounding artefacts have developed from scratch in a relatively short period of time – a few thousand years – yet the known universe is estimated to be almost fourteen billion years old.

I have stated earlier that through the technique of empathy with swarms of industrial products and by mentalizing their behaviour one can actually feel that one is living *inside* evolution. One feels the progress of evolution by observing the evolving products. For example, I enjoy looking at the development of the car species. I take pleasure in observing how technical aspects interlaced with styling aspects evolved from model to model, from the 1930 Peugeot 201 to the futuristic 208. I find it fascinating to see how the headlights evolved from separate elements into a fully embedded intelligent part of the car body.

My design universe is also composed of evolving components that live inside evolution at large. I am sensitive to the daily changing parameters that change the course of evolution, affecting the smallest constituent particles and the larger-sized products as well. I am aware of the dynamics of the inner driving force of the objects, and I can almost physically feel the continuous interaction and informative transaction between the objects. I see them behave although superficially they seem to be static. But they are not static, they only move slowly. I am aware of external forces attracting and repelling the objects, changing their visual shapes, but not the simple rules they follow to reach their visual complexity. I am also aware of the evolutionary nature of the rules themselves. Evolution is changing the rules. In all designers there should be such a sense of awareness, such an evolving design universe connected to a multitude of other universes, such a mental construct from whence one operates, that forms the home base from which architects execute their design rules.

4.7 Quantum Architecture

How can something as abstract as quantum physics possibly be instrumental in developing concepts for architectural design? At first glance this might seem highly unlikely, but the correlation between the two fields may, in fact, be quite strong. Looking back, I realize that during the past 30 years, beginning when I assisted Ilona in materializing her autonomous art works based on immediate bodily gestures, I have been working with quantum architecture without labelling it as such, without using the word.

During those years, I began in 1990 by organizing and teaching the Artificial Intuition workshops in the Aedes Gallery in Berlin and at Delft University of Technology. Then in 1991, Ilona Lénárd and I organized and taught the Global Satellite workshop during our Synthetic Dimension event in De Zonnehof in Amersfoort. In 1993, Lénárd, Rubbens, and I founded the Attila Foundation. In 1994, I invented, organized and led the international Genes of Architecture workshop. In 1996, in Rotterdam for the Rotterdam R96 Festival, I 'taught' the inflatable paraSITE web lounge to read and write environmental sounds. In 1996/1997, I applied real time behaviour to the lights and sounds of the interior installation of the Saltwater

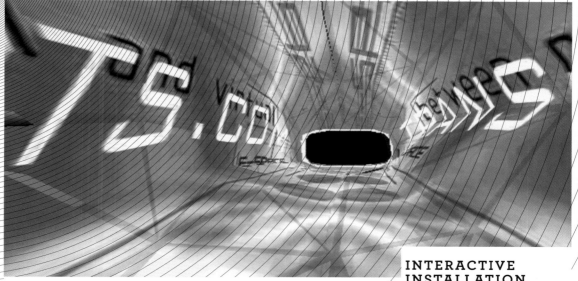

**INTERACTIVE
INSTALLATION
TRANS-PORTS
BIENNALE VENICE**
_ONL [Oosterhuis_Lénárd] 2000

Pavilion. In 1999, I presented the Trans-Ports paradigm during the first Archilab Conference in Orléans (curated by Marie-Ange Brayer and Frédéric Migayrou). In 2000, I founded Hyperbody at the Faculty of Architecture in Delft, and that same year proposed the real time behavioural pavilion Trans-Ports for the Venice Biennale of Architecture (curated by Massimilano Fuksas).

Now what made me realize that something fundamental is going on in the world around us that justifies our labelling our work and that of our peers as quantum architecture? Why is it that the Q-word so adequately describes what has been achieved? Although I knew exactly what I was doing and for what reason, I did not initially use the Q-word to describe what I was doing. In retrospect I know that the quantum aspect that I addressed is the notion of *unpredictability* and *uncertainty* of the behaviour of the smallest constituent components. From the moment I started seeing the smallest constituent components as babbling actors instead of dead static objects, I realized I was hitting on the basis of a new architecture theory. Architecture was no longer a question of composition but of behaviour; it became a matter of building relations, of informing and being informed, of processing and being processed. These in-real-time processing buildings were being animated by actors rather than being made of static objects with frozen characteristics.

The ongoing nature of processing information is a never-ending procedure, similar to the executable nature of life itself unfolding in billions of discrete steps, which can only be 'flattened' by isolating one type of information while ignoring or even destroying other types of data. Imagine a building that behaves, that is in a constant process of change and interaction with its environment and its users, a building in which all the constituent components change in real time many times per second like the flow of life itself, unfolding in discrete steps as a complex set of executable cellular automata. If you ask that kind of building what the exact geometrical position is of its nodes, you are bound to deny its

**paraSITE
WEBLOUNGE
R96 FESTIVALS
ROTTERDAM**
_ONL [Oosterhuis_Lénárd] 1996
/ Attila Foundation / photo Kas
Oosterhuis

behavioural wave functions. And that is surprisingly similar to the quantum dilemma. Once you fix the exact positions of the particles, you are bound to lose the wave patterns. Once you take the snapshot, the instance of a living process, you have manoeuvred yourself into a dead-end street from which no further development is possible. Then relations are fixed, then behaviour is dead, then all crucial streaming information has gone astray.

4.8 Irreversibility

There must be a way out of the monitoring dilemma. I felt that I needed to discuss the matter with quantum physicists so I began a discussion with Pieter Vermaas of the Faculty of Technology, Policy and Management (TPM) at Delft University of Technology. Bit by bit, I steered the dialogue towards the notion of *behaviour* in quantum mechanics. But I didn't get a positive response. It seemed to me that the world of quantum physicists has not yet entered the field of the New Kind of Science, meaning the science that considers the quantum universe to be a self-executing computation of discrete quantifiable steps, like a complex set of cellular automata. I proposed that each individual particle, as miniature as you can get, like quarks and bosons, is an individual with its own characteristics within a certain bandwidth of behavioural possibilities, similar to moving cars that stay within the white lines on the motorway. I suggested that one particle should not be seen as exactly the same as its neighbouring particle. I further suggested that I have the history of the universe on my side: not a single galaxy is the same as any other, not a single planet is the same as any other planet, not a single bird in a swarm is the same as any of the other birds, so why should atoms and electrons be viewed in such a cramped absolute way? I suggested looking at particles as dynamic information processing devices, as creative actors, exchanging information with their immediate neighbours.

HUBBLE TELESCOPE LMS 49A
_hubblesite.org

I had to come to the conclusion that the scientific field of quantum physics had not made an attempt to look at the microscopic world inside ourselves in this computational way, at least not in the scientific literature. Although scientists speak about behaviour and interaction between the particles, the behaviour is described in a mathematical equation ($\Delta x \Delta p \geq \hbar/2$ where Δx is the uncertainty in the measurement of position of a particle, Δp is the uncertainty in the measurement of momentum of the particle, and $\hbar = 6.626\mathrm{E}\text{-}34$ is Planck's constant) that presumes the interaction can be reversed, ignoring the arrow of time. It is this reversibility that Stephen Wolfram questions. Since he considers nature to be a computation and a computation cannot be set in reverse, instead it unfolds, it self-executes, it runs the simple rules of the program as it has evolved. To clarify the reversibility dilemma in one simple phrase, the behaviour of birds in a swarm is not reversible; the members of the flock are running the program. Ultimately scientists will need to rediscover the building blocks universal space is made of, and find out how planets and stars are assembled from the building blocks of space.

So I was left with my open question, which encouraged me to eventually dive deeper into this matter. It is my personal hunch that matter only feels hard and tangible because life is constructed within the bandwidth of scales that humans call their own. When you dive deep into matter you see nothing but endless limitless space. So it must be the differences in information density that decide how matter is felt by humans. Inside a soft cloud or inside hard metal one would see exactly the same infinite space. Inside atoms one would see another infinite space. I must suppose that this endlessness loops all the way back via the loose ends of the black holes, functioning as the hourglasses of time to any of the infinite number of parallel universes.

Are you still with me? Ask a physicist, read *Scientific American*. As Stephen Wolfram assumes, space might be a giant network of nodes, the nodes being informed only about the nodes they are directly connected to. Like Wolfram, I am tempted to see the

039 TOUR CYBERNÉTIQUE NICOLAS SCHÖFFER 1961

I became aware of the work of Nicolas Schöffer while living and working for a year in the Studio Van Doesburg in Meudon near Paris from September 1988 to September 1989. One year later Ilona Lénárd and I initiated the exhibition 'The Synthetic Dimension' in Museum De Zonnehof in Amersfoort, curated by Paul Coumans. De Zonnehof is a cute little building designed by Gerrit Rietveld, and accidently the neighbouring building of one of the best works of my architect father, the office building for the LEVOB insurance company. Some of the items chosen to be exhibited in 'The Synthetic Dimension' were the paintings illustrating Nicolas Schöffer's project La Ville Cybernétique. Ilona Lénárd, Paul Coumans and I went to his studio in Paris to select the works for the show. Unfortunately, Schöffer was already severely ill. His wife Eléonore Lavandeyra Schöffer showed us around and took care of the formalities for the loan of the works. In the end we were allowed to briefly enter the room where Schöffer was lying in his sickbed. He remarked that Ilona is a Hungarian name, and indeed Ilona is a native Hungarian and they chatted more than half an hour in their shared Hungarian language, which obviously was a great pleasure for him. He spontaneously donated a small painting that he made with his recently purchased Macintosh computer, which was his only way to express himself artistically since he was no longer able to draw by hand. One month later Nicolas Schöffer died. The personal encounter strengthened my respect for this innovative cybernetic artist. His early cybernetic works like the Tour Cybernétique in Liége in Belgium constructed in 1961 basically already had many of the features that current interactive art and architecture build upon. There was a 1960s' version of a computer at the base, one could literally hear the switches of the Stone Age number cruncher as it processed incoming data from the microphones and sent out modified data to the rotating light fixtures and the sound equipment. The 52-m-high Tour Cybernétique is still in place, now functioning with updated computing technology. This tower marks the beginning of interactive art in public space. Fifty years on, interactive art and architecture have become a mainstream paradigm. A simple form of interactivity is now often applied to LED façades, to fountains on public squares, to the interactive way of displaying museum pieces, supported by governmental institutes like Ars Electronica in Linz. But the best of the interactivity paradigm is yet to come. The principles of cybernetics, which pretend to be much more then flat interactivity, will be applied to complete environments, to buildings as a whole. Interactivity will evolve from the early examples of kinetic art from the 1950s and 1960s to become the genetic nature of buildings in motion. Schöffer's book La Ville Cybernétique (1969) calls for an active participation of artists and designers in the design of cities. Schöffer found that as an artist one needs to be close to the heart of the control centres, in order to influence the feel and look of society. The artist taking responsibility resonates with our view that designers should actively seek a responsible role in the collaborative design and engineering process. The designer should not be satisfied with a subordinate consultancy role alone, but take part in the financial underpinnings as well. The designer might become a cultural entrepreneur, or become an executive partner in a multidisciplinary business of designing and building larger interactive projects.

TOUR CYBER-NÉTIQUE LIÈGE NICOLAS SCHÖFFER 1961
_photo Robert Doisneau

universe as an infinitely expanding 3d cellular automaton, executing relatively simple rules, to be grasped fully by us only when we have turned all matter into information, bringing the entropy level of our universal system to almost zeroentropy being defined as the amount of information about a system that is still unknown after one has made a certain set of measurements on the system.

4.9 Design by Wire

Let's go from my layman's speculations on quantum mechanics back to quantum architecture. The notion of quantum architecture gives me the comfortable feeling that life is pleasantly unpredictable. From quantum theory I have extrapolated to the logic that smart building components will also act, as the smallest imaginable building blocks weave threads of information between their nodes. Building components are local actors executing simple rules without knowledge of the bigger flock of components around them, of which they form a part. Actors can only act locally, bound to their stage where they are performing. But again, why label this approach towards building as quantum architecture? Why not just behavioural architecture, or programmable architecture, or interactive architecture, or emotive architecture, terms I have coined earlier. I think they are all adequate in their own right, but the quantum aspect gives just a little more.

Why then should the notion of quantum be appropriate to adequately describe the 'mental state' of the in-real-time behaving building components? I think that the notion of unpredictability is the main factor, and marks the substantial difference. In a swarm of birds no one can predict exactly what each bird will do. It is like the weather, you sort of know what will come, but you cannot predict the behaviour and exact positions of all constituent particles. There are simply too many acting particles, the number-crunching process cannot be performed as an exact simulation; there are too many data to be crunched. Life can only unfold in real time, irreversibly. Life has no other choice than to self-execute. We humans can only be part of it but we can be thrilled at living inside evolution.

In the end, if one attempted a complete simulation of the universe as we know it, I strongly believe it would take exactly as long as it took the universe to be what it is here and now. Meaning that in a human lifespan one will have to work with information models that are simpler than universal reality, but not a simplified version of it. Let the model process data and instruct it to unfold to make our predictions. The quantum information model (qBIM) is not a simplification of the complex world around us, it is a new being unto itself, developing and evolving over time so as to monopolize information. The information architect must embrace a new attitude towards working with inexact data, with massive amounts of data, with changing circumstances, and with bandwidths and probability ranges rather than with discrete static data. One must learn to work within streaming models, to design on the fly, to produce while performing the design act. This can only be achieved by *designing by wire*, analogous to flying by wire and driving by wire, relying on wireless connectivity.

4.10 *Building in Motion*

Let me try to capture the importance of the quantum architecture paradigm and the necessity of designing by wire for the practice of architecture. Forward-looking practices like ONL [Oosterhuis_Lénárd] work with parametric software such as Revit Architecture, ProEngineer, Digital Project, Generative Components, Virtools (originally named Nemo, eloquently renamed into 3d as Virtools) and with the user-friendly Grasshopper/Rhino, software that supports a dynamic way of working. In the daily practice of my Delft University of Technology Hyperbody Research Group and in the protoSPACE lab we work with software packages like Virtools, MaxMSP, Arduino as well as Processing and Grasshopper. In addition, Hyperbody has found the need to develop in-house specific design tools to apply the notion of swarm behaviour in Hyperbody education, research and projects.

Inspired especially by the Virtools game design software, I quickly saw that the design process of architecture should be viewed as a developing game. Introducing the classical disciplines of architecture like styling, construction and climate design as players in a developing game, I began to see the process of designing buildings as an input > processing > output (IPO) process as well, similar to the awareness of the building bodies themselves as IPO vehicles. Developing the building information model step-by-step means directing the development towards the design of mature building bodies, ready to act and respond in the city fabric. After years of using existing and now outdated software we realized that the standards of parametric software had to be redesigned to incorporate the notion of real-time behaviour. This means that all input data should be designed to come in streaming, that all output should be sent out streaming as well, and that all crucial data should be transferred by open source technology like XML, I have come to the conclusion that the model must be a body in motion, not a fixed set of data in a static building information model. In fact I propose a new meaning for the BIM; I propose to upgrade the meaning of BIM to Bodies in Motion. In the coming decade ONL and Hyperbody researchers will investigate the relevance of the qBIM, the Quantum Building Information Model, dealing with the principles of uncertainty and unpredictability, acknowledging the emergence of the new field in architecture theory, the theory and practice of Quantum Architecture – not as a metaphor, but as acting behavioural swarm technology embedded in trans-active customized design tools.

4.11 *Living Diagrams*

One must start by building *living diagrams* that are relatively simple behavioural models, but are based on the challenging new paradigm of swarm behaviour of the locally active nodal points. One could go a step further and look at nature as it is known and see it in a different way. One could assume that matter does not exist, that there are no particles, that there are no quantum dots, at least not in the form of tangible matter. If it makes sense to think that matter does not exist then one must assume that language fools us, that traditional imagery misleads us. Just imagine diving

EMOTIVE FACTOR SALTWATER PAVILION
_ONL [Oosterhuis_Lénárd] 1997

040 EMOTIVE FACTOR SALTWATER PAVILION

Typically, the installation budget for office buildings of substantial dimensions is one third of the total construction budget. One of the most revolutionary aspects of the Saltwater Pavilion is that the installation budget, including the interactive installation, exceeded that of the pure building costs. I insisted on fully integrating the climatic installation, in order to insure a good temperature and fresh air inside the body, along with the concept of interactivity that rules the behaviour of the building body. Thus the air ducts are an integral part of the main structure and the interior design. The incoming air is tunnelled via flexible ducts from the Freshwater sector designed by Nox to the twisted floor inside my Saltwater sector. The twisted Sensorium floor functions as the air distributor for the whole space, for both the Wetlab in the lower part and for the Sensorium in the upper part. The consumed air is directed back via the narrowed elliptical shared section, using the interior of the body as the duct itself. The integrated installation components contribute to the always surprising behaviour of the Saltwater Pavilion: the cyclic airflow pumping up the airbag in front of the panoramic window in the nose, switching between daylight and artificial light every 10 minutes; the cyclic water flow forming a water tunnel every 15 minutes, challenging the public to pass under it; the massage of light and sound as directly driven by the raw data from the weather station out at sea; the virtual reality (VR) worlds projected on the polycarbonate ruled surface of the ceiling; the sensor boards that enable the public to interact with the fibreglass lights and with the ambient sounds - all experienced by the public as one encompassing and complex emotive factor.

041 SZOMBATHELY PROGRAMMABLE INTERIOR SKIN

INTER-ACTIVE SKIN WEÖRES SÁNDOR THEATRE SZOMBAT-HELY
_ONL [Oosterhuis_Lénárd] 2009

The concept of programmable buildings changing shape and content in real time is applicable to a variety of common functionalities. Knowing that the ultimate goal is to realize a fully programmable building with both a programmable structure and a programmable skin, as I foresaw a decade ago with the Trans-Ports installation during the Architecture Biennale in Venice, there are ample opportunities for practical applications of the current interaction paradigm shift. For the international competition design for the Weöres Sándor Theatre in Szombathely in Hungary (ONL, 2009), I planned a full-blown programmable interior skin. Imagine an interior skin that is constantly in motion, most of the time gently and courteously, softly and smoothly, but at times violently, harsh and with angulated movements. The behaviour of the interior would depend completely on the effects the art director imagines with the aim of intensifying the emotions staged in the performance. The flexible interior skin tiles, executed as flat, sound-absorbing cushions, are formed in real time using embedded electronic pistons. Each acoustic cushion is able to reshape itself individually. Most of the time, though, their movements are orchestrated to evoke a coherent wave pattern propagating through the whole space. The semi-soft acoustic panels can also be employed to adjust to changing acoustic needs. For some musical scores one would need a specific reflective quality. The acoustic tiles are adjusted in real time, responding to an array of sensors that measure the incoming sound waves and instruct the panels to adjust immediately.

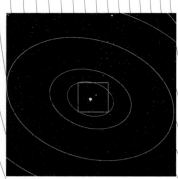

POWERS OF TEN
1977
CHARLES AND
RAY EAMES
_powersoften.com

deep into your skin, shrinking yourself to miniature proportions to look around and experience the vast space, to internalize the interior universe of vibrations that are seen and felt by carbon-based life forms as matter. The emptiness would be overwhelming, even emptier than when looking into the skies. Then one is told that there are atoms, quarks and Higgs particles. But you will soon realize that if you dove deep into the skin of those particles, you would find another really deep space. Why then depict particles as solid particles in scientific illustrations at all? Cannot the illustrators find a better way? I must insist on this issue since I want to avoid false misleading pictures that lead away from what one really wants to think. Primitive diagrams (which are like dead-end street simplifications and not at all like the vibrating world out there and in there) often prevent one from understanding how nature and processes may actually work. So, instead of static pictures one should develop *living diagrams*.

Living diagrams are executable files, executed in real time, parametric in nature, and represent a complex adaptive system that is naturally open for streaming external influences. The Virtools design tools we have been developing at Hyperbody are producing exactly that – living diagrams. A living diagram is an ongoing process that is always active, even when in seemingly stationary standby mode. A living diagram changes its visual configurations drastically when new parameters are read from a variety of linked data sources. A living diagram never stops processing, never stops breathing data in and spitting data out. A living diagram thus is also an IPO device, an actor in a swarm of connected diagrams. The smallest particles in a quantum world may be just that, living diagrams, not materialized in any sense except as observed through the human physical eye as physical entities.

The concept of the living diagram is fully synchronous with the theory of Stephen Wolfram as put forth in his book *Towards a New Science*. There have also been other physicists before him who imagined nature to be a form of real time computation, among them Stephan Hawking and Tom Stonier. In his book Wolfram disassociates himself from the myth of nature being a process of smooth flow. Instead he insists that nature is unfolding in a series of discrete steps. The scientific intuition of Wolfram thus resonates perfectly with the concept of the living diagram.

4.12 *Collaborative Design in Real Time*

In the theory of immediate architecture involving real time data exchange it is important that designers are allowed to work within a continuous work flow, within evolution at large, evolving with a massive number of discrete steps, as in computation. They must immerse themselves into the stream of an ongoing evolutionary process, where the task of the designers is to raise and 'teach' the baby BIM how to grow up to be an adult building body in a later stage of development. Since the evolving model is subject to data input from a number of orchestrated disciplines, one single designer only has partial and local control, as the project as a whole is a living evolving system, not subject to only the designer's private will. Every time one of the designers accesses the qBIM, something changes, changes that were not made by the primary designer.

In 2009, when assigning the Hyperbody MSc2 project, I gave the students the task of developing a proposal for the future laboratory of protoSPACE version 4.0. I suggested that they have six expert disciplines working together on a strictly equal basis: the structural designer, the climate designer, the materials designer, the interaction designer, the style designer, and the fabrication designer. Although I realized that there are additional contributing roles, such as the collaborative design manager, the cost expert, the traffic designer, the landscape designer, the fire expert and the light designer, I limited the project setup for practical reasons to these six disciplines. There are basically as many experts as there are well-defined design tasks. And all are, in essence, designers, so one must find a way to have them collaborate in a non-hierarchical swarm, informing their immediate neighbours only, without the need to have the overview of the design as a whole. In the MSc2 project the six defined disciplines were seen as acting forces within the evolutionary design process, the designers being the actors in the process. There would no longer be one dominant character formerly called the architect. The six designers were all architects, but each represented a different aspect of architecture. The roles were specified to clarify the scope of authority in which each of the designers felt comfortable and had expertise in. In the traditional design process most of the above roles are typically monopolized by one single person, the father figure architect at the top of the pyramid. In the new quantized design game all expert players have their own specific tasks, and are authorized to fulfil that role to the limits of their knowledge, meaning that they become true designers in their own right.

**HYPERBODY MSC2
protoSPACE 4.0**
_Hyperbody 2009

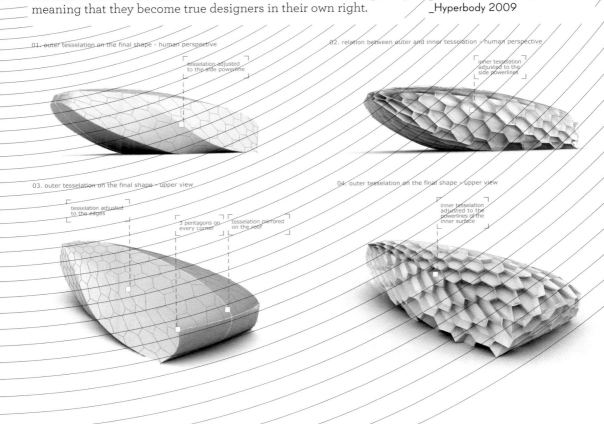

01. outer tesselation on the final shape - human perspective

tesselation adjusted to the side powerline

02. relation between outer and inner tesselation - human perspective

inner tesselation adjusted to the side powerlines

03. outer tesselation on the final shape - upper view

tesselation adjusted to the edges

3 pentagons on every corner

tesselation mirrored on the roof

04. outer tesselation on the final shape - upper view

inner tesselation adjusted to the powerlines of the inner surface

The MSc2 project showed me convincingly that the collaborative swarm-inspired process is rewarding for every player and leads to a wealth of new insights. The designers can dig much deeper into the field that is their responsibility. Their voices are heard, they feel that their presence and their expertise matters. I have also observed that it is rewarding for each to see that everyone's input is respected as active local design decisions into the larger design game. The design process becomes a collaborative process where the actors are swarming around each other rather than organized according to the traditional pyramidal structure, where the chief architect sits at the top and pulls the strings of the puppets.

And yet, what happens if there are conflicting issues that are not resolved by such a self-organizing process? Who makes the decision on how to proceed? Who disentangles a knotted process? Is there a seemingly objective computational evaluation system like Dr Hans Hubers of Hyperbody suggested in his PhD research (COLAB) on collaborative design? Can the decision-making process be automated to avoid top-down decisions?

Or should one embrace a referee system, copied directly from competitive sports games. When the referee decides that the ball is out, then the ball is out, even if it was in. When the referee decides that something is a penalty then it is a penalty even is there has not been an offense. But mind you, even here there has been technological progress that can help with the referee's decision. Computer-assisted systems have already been developed that can instantly replay the actual trajectory of the ball in three dimensions and show exactly whether that ball was in or out, or if there had been an offense or not. The system instantly informs the referee and the first decision made by the referee can be immediately adjusted on the basis of the 3d replay. In tennis, the players are allowed to ask for such an automated decision if they do not agree with the referee's decision, but as of yet no more than three times per match. Now when we consider the design process as a design game, it would not be such a bad idea to introduce the referee as another crucial expert. The role of the referee could easily be played by the client or by his or her project manager, and the client could be assisted by an automated design decision system, evaluating the proposed decisions from the individual designers.

Former Hyperbody student and former ONL trainee Dr Michael Bittermann has been working on the details of such a system to assist the design process in qualifying and quantifying design proposals, to make design decisions subject to verification on the fly. It sounds complex, but as has been explained before, complexity (as opposed to complicatedness) is not a problem as long as it is based on simple rules, and as long as it enhances the information content of newly built structures, as long as it makes them smarter, better informed, more capital intensive, as long as it pushes the profession of architectural design to a higher level, thus dropping the entropy level and raising the concise information index. At that point I can respect evaluation technologies as a progressive evolution. To complete my argument, it will then be completely useless to apply the above described techniques to buildings that are designed according to the old static paradigms, according to the old rules of mass production or worse.

Only when buildings are meant to be nonstandard and proactive will non-hierarchical swarm collaboration be relevant so as to deal with its inherent connectivity of the constituent components. The nonstandard and the immediate require knowledge and intuition of how to deal with massive amounts of streaming data.

4.13 *Massive Data*

The customized complex architecture of the nonstandard must deal with massive numbers of parameters as compared with standard architecture based on simple geometric forms. Simple forms can be computed in your head. You can easily imagine a rectangular room; you can without much effort map the idea of a rectangular form on a flat piece of paper. Conservative architects may live in Flatland without much of a problem, unaware of Spaceland. But your brains are not capable of computing massive amounts of data and thus cannot compute complex shapes that easily, since they are described by thousands of vertexes that must be organized by communicating brain cells. An *idiot savant* might be able to memorize thousands of numbers of a telephone book or memorize thousands of different coordinates, but these data would not be translated into a coherent structure. For the non-standard architecture one has to deal with the many in a new way, in a joint trans-active operation between oneself and one's computing devices. One needs to accept the fact that tons of data will have to be processed for any information-rich project, both in the design process and in its intended life as a functioning building.

Interestingly enough, traditional architects usually appreciate nature, appreciating the thousands of different leaves on the tree as if this was normal. In reality this is the effect of nature acting as a computing device executing simple rules to create this kind of complexity. If this can be appreciated so easily by conservative designers, it should not be threatening for them to appreciate the inherent complexity of the nonstandard. Neither should one question the necessity of dealing with massive amounts of data to generate complexity. Nor should one be opposed to the idea of proactive structures feeding on massive amounts of data in real time. Nor should one be afraid of the transaction programs for collaborative design in real time to crunch and produce massive amounts of data. Nothing is more natural than that if one is able to profit from the new wealth, if one does not feel intimidated by unfamiliar technology. One must learn to take advantage of the new abundance by diving into the deep sea and learning to swim. That will be the only way to avoid feeding one's defensive system, to avoid turning one's back on the progressively complex world of today, to avoid looking at the world of today through the rear-view mirror.

To summarize in a few words, complexity is beautiful, intrinsic complexity and the massive amount of data generated by the nonstandard and the immediate is beautiful. Whereas mass production was once beautiful, now it is the unique products of the process of industrial customization that will be thought to be beautiful and will be the key to locally reversing the Second Law of Thermodynamics. Starting here and now.

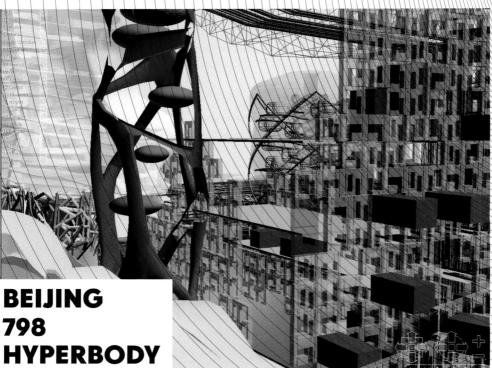

BEIJING 798 HYPERBODY MSC1

_Hyperbody 2006 /
SEUARCH Nanjing

042 BEIJING 798

For Hyperbody's MSc1 2008 design course I gave the students a few simple but strict rules on the basis of which they could develop their individual sectors. I supplied them with a boundary condition in the form of a spherical envelop with a diameter of 400 m, composed of 24 spatially interlocking pieces, like the pieces of a three-dimensional puzzle. Each student was assigned to design one of the 24 pieces. One of the main procedural design instructions I gave them was to communicate only with their immediate neighbours, without pursuing any attempt to get an overview of the total ball. The mutual neighbours were instructed to exchange sets of data, data they needed from their neighbours and data they would be happy to secrete, in any form, such as information, liquid, forces, gases. All data are considered to be subject to a process of bilateral negotiations. The exchanged data form the parameters for the individual designs. The rule is to negotiate with your immediate neighbours only, and with one neighbour at a time, one on one communication only, peer to peer. If each student indeed obeys that rule, the urban design concept implies that the sphere will self-assemble from the bottom up to form a consistent three-dimensional city. The students act like the innocent but expert birds in a swarm, following their simple rules, but eventually making up the complex shape and the complex surprising behaviour of that swarm. The bottom-up development of the 24 individual pieces on the basis of a few simple but strong rules has proven to be an effective format for a large-scale urban design project. I intend to apply this concept to real life commissions for urban planning studies.

043 CATALUNYA CIRCUIT CITY

I chose 'Speed and Friction' as the theme of a one-week workshop I was invited to lead by director Alberto Estevez of the ESARQ University in Barcelona in the year 2004. A swarm of 250 students participated, with the assistance of an expert flock of 14 international and ONL plus Hyperbody tutors. The design brief I gave was to redesign the Catalunya Formula I Circuit into Catalunya Circuit City. Fourteen groups of students were assigned to each design one particular sector of the circuit. I gave them a few basic rules, of which I will recall the most important rule here. I instructed the students to communicate with their immediate neighbours only, to process the flow of energy, of traffic, people, waste and information from their immediate neighbours only, and to secure that the flow is permanently sustained. This implied that in total 14 sectors, each of them adopting one of the curves of the track, were bilaterally linked to each other, developed highly individually, yet forming a coherent whole. The 14 sectors represented the connected building bodies on the scale of a city. I told the students and their tutors not to worry about the overall picture, since that was already taken care of by that one simple rule. Worrying about the overall picture would be counterproductive, and against swarm logic. No one in the swarm worries about the overall shape of their swarm. Just like you step into your car, the citizens of the sectors would enter sideways, step into the flow, and become part of Catalunya Circuit City without overseeing the whole, but definitively feeling part of the propulsive excitement of the 14 connected sectors of the looped circuit, transformed into an intense city.

CATALUNYA CIRCUIT CITY BARCELONA
_ONL [Oosterhuis_Lénárd] 2004 / Hyperbody / ESARQ

4.14 New Kind of Building

The New Kind of Building is based on the extreme individualiza-
tion of the building components to the maximum level of detail,
in combination with an extreme 'socialization' of the factors
driving the tagged components. You have seen that the tagged
components must be designed and labelled according to the
principles of nonstandard architecture and produced according to industrial CNC-driven customization procedures. You
have seen that the tagged building components constitute the
synthetic building body, a body that desperately needs style.
Personal design universes will act upon the raw design material,
swarming like oscillating nodes in weightless space, waiting to
be shaped by powerlines. Internal swarm logic rules, but is subject to parametric input imposed on the swarm from outside the
design system. The organized point cloud of reference points
waits to be the subject of an opinion on the curvature of the feature lines, expecting an opinion on the double-curved surfaces
for the transition from one instance to the other.

I have initiated the development of prototypes such as the
Festo Interactive Wall and the Dynamic Sound Barrier concept
for Breda to show the potential of tagged and informed building
components being informed by their immediate neighbours. The
immediate processes unfolding both in the design process and
in the real time behaviour are administered in the quantumBIM,
the preferred model for collaborative design and engineering
during the complete lifecycle. The road has been cleared for
nonstandard design and for the new aesthetics of the new kind
of building, alongside industrial customization that allows for
the production of uniquely shaped building components and
their assembly into complex spatial compounds. Embedding
miniature robotic brains and actuators into the built structures
weaves a new relationship between users and their immediate
environment.

You have seen how building bodies are alien spaceships negotiating with local actors to establish a meaningful relationship
with the building site (just that). You have seen that the building
components are packed to go from the CNC machines and to
be assembled at the building site at the very moment they are
needed (just then). You have seen that the individual building
components fit only in one place since they are all unique in size
and shape (just there). You have learned that the data exchange
between environment and tagged building components must
unfold in real time to insure an accurate response to changing
circumstances. I have pointed out that it is mandatory to exchange data in real time between the various experts to increase
quality design, and to 'teach' the building bodies to operate on a
higher level of intelligence (just so).

Because data have the internal drive to run the cellular automata, they are bound to inform a variety of interacting complex
adaptive systems. Interaction is a dialogue, a form of socializing
of tagged groups of cells, ranging from tagged atoms and molecules to large tagged building bodies and trans-active city systems. This is the logical consequence of the predictable future of

FLOATING PAVILION YEOSU WORLD EXPO

_ONL [Oosterhuis_Lénárd] 2009

buildings in motion, the evolution of data that do not want to be trapped in a dead-end alley. To quote Kevin Kelly: *If you are not in real time you're dead*. Buildings will be designed to move all the time, balancing their bodies to come to a complete standstill, like the mile-high skyscraper in Saudi Arabia, or to proactively trigger the imagination of the public by its seductive mobility as in the Dynamic Acoustic Barrier project. The choice is between one dimensional static architecture and multimodal dynamic architecture. The choice is yours.

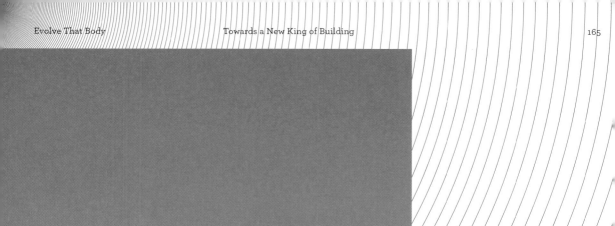

**CET
BUDAPEST**
_ONL [Oosterhuis_Lénárd]
2007-2011

**47° 29' 1'' N
19° 03' 40'' E**

044 GÖMBÖC

The large 2.5-m-high Gömböc inside the Hungarian Pavilion at the Shanghai World Expo is made of polished stainless steel. The meaning of Gömböc in Hungarian is something like 'fatty'. A Gömböc is a special mathematically defined three-dimensional object that has two equilibrium points, one stable and one unstable. If placed on a horizontal surface in an arbitrary position the Gömböc returns to the stable equilibrium point, similar to Weeble toys. While the egg-shaped Weebles rely on a weight in the bottom, the Gömböc consists of homogenous material all over, thus the shape itself accounts for self-righting. The stable point is not the feature of the Gömböc I am interested in, it is of course the unstable equilibrium point that I am particularly obsessed by. The single unstable equilibrium point of the Gömböc is on the opposite side of the stable side. It is possible to balance the body in this position, but the slightest disturbance makes it fall back to the stable point. The existence of a Gömböc-type object was posed by the Russian mathematician Vladimir Arnold at a conference in 1995, in a conversation with Hungarian mathematician Gábor Domokos, who designed the Shanghai version of the Gömböc together with architect Péter Várkonyi, also from Hungary. The reason that this fatty odd-shaped volume is of interest to me is that with programmable actuator technology we would be able to modify the shape of such an object in real time, thereby changing the position of the equilibrium point dynamically. Thus we would be able to stabilize the instability and destabilize the stability at will. Transferring the knowledge of how to achieve this to the world of architecture means that a substantial building could be developed to find itself in a permanent state of instability without falling. The consequences are humongous and utterly relevant, one could literally design a pyramid standing upside down without tipping over.

GÖMBÖC HUNGARIAN PAVILION SHANGHAI EXPO

_expo2010.cn /
photo Kas Oosterhuis

045 DYNAMIC SOUND BARRIER

DYNAMIC SOUND BARRIER
_ONL [Oosterhuis_Lénárd] 2009

There is only a barrier when you need one. In its non-informed position the wings of the sound barrier are stretched flat on either side of the railway track, leaving open views from one sector of the city of Breda to the other sector on the other side of the elevated railway. A permanent sound barrier would block this open view. In 2009, the ONL design team developed a proposal for a dynamic barrier that leaves the view open when there are no trains passing. When a train comes close, a sensor notices its presence and sends a signal to raise the first wing to absorb the sound when the train is at that particular position. Each wing informs the next, synchronized in real time with the speed of the train by an additional array of sensors. A wave effect similar to that of the popular public wave in football stadiums will be the spatial effect of the individual wings informing their neighbouring wings one by one, in sync with the speed of the train. The wings are connected to each other by a flexible sound-absorbing fabric and thus insure a coherent soundproof barrier, but only when and where there is a train. Once the train has passed, the wings lower their position again one by one and smoothly return to their horizontal arrangement. Inside the wings there are a few electronic pistons to actuate the contraction of the wing to move up. This concept of a dynamic sound barrier serves as an example for the vast sustainable potential of informed and tagged building components. This strategy will naturally apply to those situations where there is a temporary need for a separating membrane between two conflicting conditions.

4.15 *Tweets for a New Kind of Building*

Radicalize the concept - The radical concept contains precise qualitative and quantitative data and is described in a few lines of script.

Start with a point cloud - The point cloud of reference points forms the personal universe of the designer.

Draft simple rules - Simple rules drive the reference points to communicate with their immediate neighbours.

Internalize swarm logic - The flock of nodal points behaves from bottom-up to become the members of the swarm of building components.

Insert powerlines - Powerlines inform and top-down organize a selection of nodes to shape the feature lines of the swarm.

Conceive a complex adaptive system - The interacting members of the swarm of building components form a complex adaptive system.

Build an input/output device - The complex adaptive system is an input/output device processing information from outside the system.

Shape the building body - An input processing output device makes a building body have a consistent body plan.

Apply parametric design - A building body is modelled as a relational set of building components subject to external and internal parameters.

Work in a digital paperless office - In the digital paperless office the design evolves exclusively in the 3d model. Two-dimensional drawings are abstract derivatives and contain incomplete, inexact and hence false and misleading information.

Establish a building information model (BIM) - The building components and their parameters are directed by the earliest conceptual idea in a building information model which is then continuously updated.

Exchange data bilaterally - The members of a swarm of design experts exchange data bilaterally.

Choose your field of expertise - In the design swarm there is no leader, every expert makes decisions in their own field of expertise.

Program the body plan - The three-dimensional body plan is the outcome of a complex process of imposed external parameters balanced out with the body's internal drivers.

Map interacting populations - The organized informed reference points populate the double curved surfaces of the body.

Synchronize structure and skin - The dimensions of the structure and the skin of the body are synchronized since they evolve from one system.

One building, one detail - The populated surface enveloping the body as one continuous consistent skin carries a consistent parametric detail that adapts to the different positions on the skin.

Specify the detail - Specifying the parametric nodal detail allows adaptation to local conditions to achieve different features and functions.

Include ornamentation - Ornamentation is included in the specified synchronized structure-plus-skin system.

Fuse different disciplines - The different disciplines of art, music, graphic design, architecture, engineering and fabrication are naturally fused digitally.

Apply collaborative design and engineering - As the protoBIM evolves, the geometry from the designer and the calculations from the engineer speak the same computing language.

Appreciate multiplicity - The fusion process of collaborative design and engineering leads to a natural complexity and multiplicity of function and meaning.

Transform - The body plan features seamless transformations from one constituent building section to the other.

Perform emotive styling - The styling of the building body is provided with emotive factors that enhance their participatory relationship with the users.

Embed tags - All constituent building components are tagged and can be addressed individually (when the tags are small processing brains they can be addressed in real time).

Practice file-to-factory - From the BIM, each individual component's dimensions and performance is described exactly to facilitate the file-to-factory production process, using the data directly to drive the CNC machines.

Familiarize yourself with nonstandard geometry - The mathematics of nonstandard geometry dealing with the infinite enables one to describe and manipulate double curved surfaces.

Exploit nonstandard architecture - Nonstandard architecture exploits the new frontiers created by nonstandard mathematics.

Think inclusively - Nonstandard logic is inclusive as it can describe all possible shapes, including simple platonic forms.

Work with high precision - Nonstandard architecture requires high precision in the definition of both concept and geometry.

Radicalize customization - Radical industrial customization allows for the design of nonstandard buildings in which all building components are unique in shape and size.

Switch to a Design and Build practice - Nonstandard designs linked to CNC production make possible Design and Build contracts in which the designer takes substantial responsibility for the exactness of the data while the builder insures the transparency of costs.

Stream real time behaviour - Building components that are informed in real time, that process information and emit modified data are the participating building blocks for real time behaviour of dynamic building bodies.

Parametrize multimodality - Buildings behaving in real time can have multimodal functioning, transforming from one operational mode to another by changing the parametric values that drive the structure and interior/exterior skin.

Develop living diagrams - Since static diagrams give a false picture of a dynamic process, one must instead model living diagrams using game development platforms.

Think of your building as an instrument - The informed building is a vehicle in which to go places, as an instrument to be played by its users.

BIM is Building In Motion - A building that changes shape and content in real time is a dynamic building in motion.

Program the motion - Buildings in motion can be addressed in real time and programmed to transform into a variety of functional modes.

Prepare for proactivity - Buildings that are programmed to transform may develop a will of their own and proactively propose changes themselves.

Use the ground in multiple ways - Multiplicity and multimodality naturally allows the merger of different functions, with one function embedded in the other, leading to a multiple and sustainable use of the ground.

Start a dialogue with the alien - Establish a dialogue in the form of streaming data exchange between the evolving extraterritorial qBIM and the local climatic and ground conditions.

Enter the transaction space - The exhibition space as well as the building site is a transaction space, generating massive amounts of data.

Acknowledge that repetition no longer equals beauty - Mass production made repetition beautiful and a dominant aesthetic but industrial customization brings this to an end.

Dive into diversity - Diversity is the natural aesthetic of nonstandard design linked to industrial customization.

Repetition is no longer sustainable - Mass production of building components for the building catalogue is no longer sustainable since it produces even when there is no demand.

TORS
L, *v* ARNHEM
_ONL [Oosterhuis_Lénárd] 1993

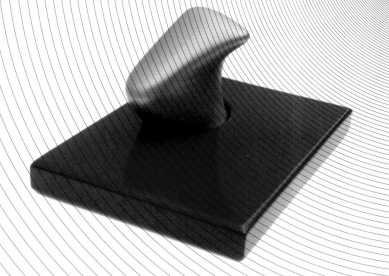

46 TORS

Although imagined and designed back in 1993 for the 'L,v' exhibition in Arnhem curated by Hans Veldhuizen, the TORS concept is still an exemplary design for nonstandard architecture, for inherent customization, for an informed main structure. Ilona and I were in the early days of our joint pursuit of the fusion of art and architecture. The TORS sculpture building is intended to be a building of over 60 m in height, containing 20 floors including the basement levels, streamlined to save on cooling and heating costs. The interior elliptical atrium space, which transforms from floor to floor, is imagined to be populated all the way up by an abundance of oxygen-producing plants, contributing to the clean air inside the air conditioning system. The TORS torso as a whole balances in a bowl-shaped building pit, clearly showing that the foundations of any building must be part of the overall design. The TORS body theoretically wobbles in the concave pit, maintaining its active balance. There was no technology available at that time to realize the TORS concept in all of its advanced aspects, but it is feasible now, after 20 years of progressive experience in practice. The for nonstandard designs mandatory file-to-factory technology is now, in 2010, well developed via projects like the Cockpit and the iWEB, green building is definitively on the political agenda, and above all it has been proven via prototypes such as the NSA Muscle, the Muscle Body, the Interactive Tower, the Festo Interactive Wall, and by the provocative but 100 per cent realistic proposal for the Dynamic Barrier, that embedded actuator technology is now ready to facilitate the balancing act of a permanent instability.

Produce on demand - Nonstandard architecture leads naturally to production on demand; building components are produced in one form to fit in one place at one time for one reason.

Merge - The concise merger of concept, style, structure, and material is the natural condition of nonstandard logic.

Impose personal style - Personal style is imposed on the parametric building body to enhance the emotional attachment of the users to the customized products.

Sculpt your building - Buildings turn into autonomous sculptures by closing the door, sculptures turn into functional buildings by opening the door.

Empower powerlines - Powerlines impose their power on the swarm of reference points, forming the boundary conditions for the nonstandard geometry.

Sketch intuitively - Intuitive sketches drawn by fast hand movements or registered by a 3d digitizer can function as the trajectories of the powerlines.

Attract or repel - The powerlines either attract or repel the points of the point cloud of reference points.

Build your building body - The building needs a coherent body composed of hundreds of thousands of unique components, each with an internal drive to perform.

Form a 3d puzzle - The building body is like a 3d puzzle of interlocking components, unique in their size, shape and behaviour.

Vectorize the body - The building body naturally becomes a vectorial body since the body has an internal drive to go places.

Enter sideways - In the vectorial body there is no front entrance; users step into the body via the side entrance in order to participate in a virtual journey, to go places.

Insert the inlay - Groups of building components are conceived as smoothly embedded inlays in larger structures, ensuring the continuity of the whole body.

Build spaceships - Building bodies are conceived in weightless digital space until they are informed with gravity and when their parametric BIM is always open for information on local conditions.

Reduce the footprint - Building bodies conceived as spaceships in digital space typically have a reduced footprint and thus touch the earth lightly, minimizing foundation costs. Landed spacecraft with small footprints typically feature large cantilevered parts jutting from the body.

Design monocoque structures - The building bodies of monocoque structures are constructed with load-bearing shells, or a spatial system of structural cells, thus avoiding columns, beams and other half-products from the building catalogue.

Compose your project-specific building catalogue - Any nonstandard building body creates its own unique catalogue of building components, highly systematic in itself, but not standardized for use in other building bodies.

Constitute diagrid structures - Diagrid structures are used to describe double curved surfaces that constitute the structural system for load bearing shells. These shells have increased structural efficiency compared to square gridded systems.

Distribute gravity - Diagrid systems distribute the gravity forces and wind forces along the curvature of the surface much better than does a vertical column and beam grid utilizing additional stabilizers.

Use basic materials - The project-specific building catalogue allows for minimal handling of basic materials, thus reducing the need to adjust the cutting, bending, or assembly of mass-produced materials.

Do not waste - Industrial customization guarantees a significant reduction in the waste that ensues when adjustments must be made to materials on the building site, since all the building components are prepared individually at the factory and then packed to be assembled at one specific spot in the structure.

Design and build only once - The building body design strategy insures that the building is built only once, modelled in one evolving BIM, produced without molds, assembled without scaffolding.

Compact the body - Vectorial building bodies typically are built compactly, featuring rounded-off body corners with few limbs sticking out, similar to most other product bodies.

Improve the volume/surface ratio - Nonstandard designs tend to have a more efficient volume/surface ratio as compared to modernist square designs.

Increase the potato index - The potato index maps the invested capital of the body in euros/kilogram of material as compared to the market price of potatoes; the higher the potato index the better informed the building body has been.

Streamline - Building bodies with an explicit vector are streamlined to improve aerodynamics, reducing high wind speeds at the corners, thus reducing heat loss and reducing cooling needs.

Make flood-proof - Self-supporting shell structures with a reduced footprint are naturally flood-proof since they typically are positioned above the ground or are capable of floating if subjected to upward water pressure.

Make hurricane proof - This seems not important in our (European) region, but is relevant since strong winds have no grip on streamlined bodies.

Participate - The transition from our consumer society to a participatory society allows every person to be an active player in the collaborative design game, and every object becomes an active player in the swarm of building components.

Become an actor - As cars are actors on the elaborately branched motorway system, similarly buildings are actors in the complex adaptive city fabric.

Nature is computation - Nature is essentially a computational system, executing complex interacting sets of cellular automata in real time, computing discrete steps unfolding in time units as small as femtoseconds or even attoseconds.

Deploy game theory - Game theory is a branch of applied mathematics used in the social sciences and also is the basis of swarm design strategies and real time behaviour of proactive building bodies.

Evolve new species - The evolution of building bodies leads to the birth of new building species, as in the vectorial body with its vectorized body plan.

Learn to work with massive amounts of data - Nonstandard design strategies and streaming buildings in motion require the processing of massive amounts of data.

Become an information architect - The information architect can deal with massive amounts of streaming data, and can, in real time, balance top-down control and bottom-up behaviour of the constituent components of the building bodies.

Other Books by the Author:

Artificial Intuition | *co-authors: Konrad Wohlhage (introduction)* | 1989, Aedes

City Fruitful | *co-authors: Ashok Bhalotra, Adri Huisman, Willem Schuringa* | 1992, 010 Publishers | ISBN 90 6450 179 3

Sculpture City | *co-authors: Ilona Lénárd, Menno Rubbens* | 1994, 010 Publishers | ISBN 90 6450 229 3

Kas Oosterhuis Architect/Ilona Lénárd Visual Artist | *co-authors: Ilona Lénárd, Bernard Cache (introduction), Marcos Novak (email discussion)* | 1998, 010 Publishers | ISBN 90 6450 298 6

Kas Oosterhuis Programmable Architecture | *co-author: Ole Bouman (introduction)* | 2000, l´Arcaedizioni | ISBN 88 7838 103 9

Kas Oosterhuis Emotive Architecture | *inaugural speech Delft University of Technology* | 2001, 010 Publishers | ISBN 90 6450 501 2

Kas Oosterhuis Architecture Goes Wild | 2002, 010 Publishers ISBN 90 6450 409 1

BCN Speed and Friction | *co-author: Alberto Estevez (introduction)* | 2004,, SITES books ESARQ | ISBN 0 930829 53 0

Hyperbodies Towards an E-motive Architecture | 2003, Birkhäuser | ISBN 3 7643 6969 8

Game Set and Match | *co-author: Ole Bouman (introduction), participants conference* | 2003, BK TU Delft | ISBN 90 5269316 1

Game Set and Match II | *co-author: Hyperbody and participants conference* | 2006, Episode Publishers | ISBN 90 5973 036 4

ONL Hyperbody Logic | 2007, AADCU China | ISBN 7 5434 6164 1

751 Multiplayer Design Studio | *co-author: Hyperbody* | 2008, CABP China | ISBN 978 7 112 10281 5

iA#1 | *co-authors: ONL, Hyperbody* | 2007, Episode Publishers | ISBN 978 90 5973 058 8

iA#2 | *co-authors: ONL, Hyperbody* | 2009, Episode Publishers | ISBN 978 90 5973 062 5

ONLogic Speed and Vision | *co-author: Philip Jodidio (introduction)* | 2009, Images Publishing | ISBN 99 781864 702866

iA#3 | *co-authors: ONL, Hyperbody* | 2010, Jap Sam Books | ISBN 978 94 90322 08 3